AF572394

SHALOM IS . . . WHOLE COMMUNITY

BY JOAN ARNOLD

A SHALOM RESOURCE
PUBLISHED FOR JOINT EDUCATIONAL DEVELOPMENT
UNITED CHURCH PRESS, PHILADELPHIA

This book is one of four adult primers on shalom, edited by Charles McCollough. Other primer titles are:

Economics and the Gospel
Waging Peace—A Way Out of War
Next Steps Toward Racial Justice

A list of acknowledgments appears on pp 137–145.

Joint Educational Development—an ecumenical partnership for the development of educational systems and resources. Christian Church (Disciples of Christ), Cumberland Presbyterian Church, Episcopal Church, Evangelical Covenant Church, Moravian Church, Presbyterian Church in the United States, Reformed Church in America, United Church of Canada, United Church of Christ, United Presbyterian Church in the U.S.A.

Library of Congress Cataloging in Publication Data

Arnold, Joan, 1929–
Shalom is . . . whole community.
(A Shalom resource)
"Published for Joint Educational Development."
Bibliography: p.
1. Community. I. Title.
HM131.A75 261.8 75-22492
ISBN 0-8298-0298-3

PREFACE

There is a need to speak of God's revelation from a woman's perspective. For us, as women, patriarchal interpretations of the Bible fall short and do not always speak from and to our experience. In this book I want to emphasize the mothering, the sistering, the befriending, the challenging, the empowering, and the all-embracing nature of God. That is a knowledge that we come to as we love and accept a wider variety of experience. I believe women can bring this wider perspective to biblical interpretation.

I want us women to develop a theology of power that communicates life. Instead of understanding power only as domination and destructiveness, I want to explore the experience and gift of power as spirit, as energy and love. This kind of communicative and persistent power, especially when wielded by women, could flesh out our ideas of nonviolence, which sometimes connotes something purely negative, a kind of unwillingness to act. Christian theology has so far not had a theology of power, and thus has accepted secular and exclusively male definitions of power more or less uncritically. As Spirit, God *gives us power* to act in love; as Christians, we are called to *communicate power* to others without fear.

I appeal to women, as to members of other minority groups also, to work toward transforming the old world in which we find ourselves. We as women *can* take responsibility in the power of the Spirit in the public world as leaders, as mothers, as sisters, to bring life and trust where there is now fear and death. Because our feelings of sympathy and empathy are closer to the surface, we can help men free themselves to feel and to "feel with" the sufferings of the world and to overcome them in a new vision of shalom as whole, inclusive community.

Shalom for us in the United States will include not only women's perspective but also Black liberation theology as well as Latin American liberation theology. Until we can hear what our Black brothers and sisters are saying to us, until we can end segregation in housing and schooling and meet each other face to face, we do not have a whole community of shalom. Until our churches are communities that can encourage a rich plurality of peoples and their cultures, we have not yet begun seriously as a community of equals to work at shalom.

I would like to thank all the people whose conversation with me has entered into this book. There is my mother, Dr. Magda Arnold, who functioned as a model of a loving woman and as a scholar of integrity; my husband and friend, Gilbert Romero, who has been both supporter and consultant at many points for this book. My thanks go also to the members of the Philadelphia Theological Community (now reconstituted as Colloquy of Reston), especially to Dr. Richard Shaull and Dr. Bruce Boston, who discussed many of these ideas and made valuable suggestions. I don't know how to thank the patience of the editor, Dr. Charles McCollough, who has been alternately stimulating and patient, and whose theological questioning has pushed me to an increasing awareness of how we reflect theologically in today's world.

I owe a special debt of gratitude to the great-souled women who met at Grailville in the summer of '72, in a group called Woman Exploring Theology. It was in that group that I began to see what it might mean to do theology out of our experience as women.

I should also like to thank my colleagues at United Theological Seminary, who have provided continuing conversation and community over this past year. This experience has been both confirmation of and going beyond what can be written down.

All these people and their communities have been for me signs of shalom. I hope this book may communicate a little of that to you.

August, 1974

Joan Arnold
United Theological Seminary
Dayton, Ohio

CONTENTS

INTRODUCTION

A BOOK ABOUT COMMUNITY

Community in the dictionary is defined as a body of people with something in common. We are concerned about a particular kind of community, one that is whole, that is in harmony, together, fair, just, peaceful, sharing and fulfilling for its members. The something-in-common for our particular community is a vision of shalom given by God and revealed in the Old Testament and the New Testament. The way to shalom is by breaking down the "dividing wall of hostility" (Ephesians 2:14) and making our communities whole. In this book we will discuss *community as a body of people with biblical shalom in common,* and we will explore how this kind of community can be built. We will present six separate groupings (church, sexual, family, work, city, and world communities). We will ask: How can they become whole? How can hostility, wars, and injustice be overcome? How can we build shalom communities?

First, we will dream a dream; we will set forth a vision of shalom so that we will know what we are looking for. This vision includes abundant life, liberation, public peace, a bias toward the poor, and democratic decision-making. Then we will suggest a method for achieving this vision. This method has six steps: naming, analyzing, envisioning, acting, reflecting, and following through. Next, we will employ this method as we seek to overcome the walls of hostility in our sexual role definitions and in the problems of families. Finally, after suggesting some approaches to building whole communities in our personal and interpersonal lives, we will broaden our scope and ask, How can we work for shalom in our jobs, in our cities, and in our world?

THE NEED FOR SHALOM

Shalom is whole community. The idea is as old as Yahweh's promise to the people of Israel and has as much grace and promise today as it had then. Like the children of Israel long ago, like our foremothers and forefathers who came to this country attempting to fashion a new life, we too are called out of ourselves into a new time, called to begin a new work.

Shalom community requires both the ability to dream and to start out afresh. It requires looking at our lives, evaluating them, and seeing how we can overcome the isolation that has somehow become a basic pattern for most of us. How can we go beyond where we are in the separateness of our lives as individuals, where our families are often fearful about each other and about the world beyond? How can we move into community, into new orders that enable us to grow and create and finally build a world of shalom?

Community is a building process that begins again with each new generation. It begins with a mutual willingness to have a dialogue, not just to talk at one another. Dialogue is a shared process of interaction, reflection, and action. It leads us to create community and concern through our work, through our understanding of ourselves and one another beyond our sex and work roles, and through our participation in and building of the city and of the larger world. In community we can also work at ways to make the resources of our world more available to fill people's needs, not to use them wastefully and greedily for ourselves. Out of the experiences of community building, we learn to celebrate our shared joys and sorrows, the shared struggle and the small victories along the way.

Shalom is whole community, a promise, a vocation, a hope, and a celebration. The future is open in two ways. We can let the world drift so that we become more and more separated from those who differ from us—rich from poor, Black from white, women from men, old from young; or we can begin to break down the walls of hostility and develop communities of caring and concern where we take responsibilities for one another as brothers and sisters. One way is the way of Cain; the other is the way of Abel.

BEING MYSELF IN COMMUNITY

When we qualify community with the biblical concept of shalom, we affirm a paradox of personal and communal strength. In a creative community, individuals grow in their own personal strength and uniqueness, and the community serves this goal at the same time that it empowers the group of individuals to act in unison. Shalom requires personal justice as well as community peace.

My personal struggle has been one of gaining my own strength in various communities and separate from them. I have experienced my own life as a discovery of who I am, a learning to be myself, to set my own goals. I have needed communities to help me set my goals in life, not to set my goals for me.

Many years of my life were dependent years, as a student, as a teaching sister in a religious order, and always as a woman in a society where dependency is a woman's assigned role. It has been a struggle for me to become my own woman. Part of the struggle has been against patterns of domination, where people followed traditional community customs and manners that put me down. But a good part of the struggle has been against myself—learning to risk myself by taking responsibility for doing things I had never done before. Some of it has been a process of learning to do things on my own; some of it has been seeing women both older and younger than myself who have been good examples and companions. I have also been fortunate in meeting men who have been able to encourage me, as I hope I have encouraged them, in the struggle to become free of old male-female stereotypes.

My husband, Gilbert Romero, an Old Testament scholar, has been the most understanding of all. Our relationship over the years has been one of friendship, warmth, affection, and a continuous sharing of ideas. His concerns for the political theology of the Old Testament have meshed and struck sparks with my study of Latin American theology.

What I am as a theologian is colored by my life-style, by the integration of thought, feeling and action that I have begun to achieve. Thus, my theology is intimately related to action, both on the private and on the public level. For me, theology is more a discovery of the word of God spoken to us today toward the future than it is a study of past theological systems. As a theologian, my reflection, writing, politics, and prayer are directed to the concerns of women and to oppressed people all over the world, particularly in the Latin American countries.

For the past two years, I have been a part of a community of eight adults and three children struggling toward an alternative style of community and work. In the Philadelphia Theological Community, our primary goals have been two: to work at job alternatives both for ourselves and for others, and to create a style of family living open to the larger community. The Community has always taken the position that it is important to define one's goals for oneself—to know what each of us wants to do—so that together, in community, we could figure out how to accomplish these goals.

In particular, the second chapter of this book has grown out of the educational work that a number of us in the Philadelphia Theological Community have done together. Originally our procedure was called the "Freire Method" because it was inspired by the work of Paulo Freire, an educator from Brazil who now works for the World Council of Churches. The method is very much in line with our own purpose, because it offers a way of helping people to clarify their own goals and wishes with respect to work, marriage, sex roles, and the like. This book has grown out of ongoing discussions we have had among ourselves and with other people as we have dealt with practical community problems and tried to apply a liberating approach to solving them.

In the Theological Community, our theological concerns have been both practical and biblical. Above all, however, the sustained reflection and conversation that have gone into this book have meant a reliving of the gospel as good news, as a new possibility of shalom in a world tragically shadowed by "limited" wars, by the threat of nuclear warfare, and by oppression all over the world. Of the many rich aspects of shalom, I have isolated a few for guidance through this book. *A whole community of shalom means: (1) abundance, (2) liberation, (3) a public peace (not only private), (4) a strong bias toward the poor and dispossessed, and (5) decentralized or democratic uses of power.* I will briefly explore two partially conflicting views of shalom in the traditions of King David and Moses to illustrate the fifth meaning of shalom.

SHALOM IN THE BIBLE

Abundant Life

In the Bible we are invited to dream of abundant life on earth. But this abundant life does not happen without risk, nor does it happen for one person in isolation. The real test of abundance is whether it can be shared, whether it gives life to others.

Liberation

Shalom in the Bible is also liberation, a struggle to take up the responsibility for our own lives and for our communities. It is a struggle for freedom—freedom that is spiritual, personal, and *political.* Freedom is for all or for none. Freedom for some at the expense of others is domination, not liberation.

A number of contemporary theologians are speaking today of the process of Christian action in the world as a process of the powerless taking power. The word for that process is "liberation," which has its roots in the Old Testament story of the freeing from slavery and oppression. Liberation is a process of human development *with others,* not at the expense of others. The key question is always, "What will this course of action mean for other people, for different groups of people?" A theology of liberation rejects the false peace of the uncontested domination of the privileged at the expense of others.

Public Peace

The Old Testament ideal of peace and prosperity was based on the liberation from slavery of a whole nation. It was not only a private freedom. It meant that the little band of homeless people from Egypt was able to find a place to live and work—a place whose resources were plentiful and available to all. It was a place where people did not have to live as slaves privately or publicly. Even in Old Testament times, however, not all became prosperous. But Yahweh, their God, was concerned for the poor and expressed his concern both in the writings of the law and through the word of the prophets. This was illustrated in the notion of a jubilee year.

Bias Toward Poor

By law every seventh year was to be a kind of sabbath year, specifically a year of replenishment of natural resources. The land was to be allowed to lie fallow and to rest. God has always been the great ecologist—and the great giver of welfare. Every seven weeks of years, that is, every fiftieth year, was the supreme year of jubilee:

> And you shall hallow the fiftieth year, and proclaim liberty throughout the land to all its inhabitants; it shall be a jubilee for you, when each of you shall return to his property and each of you shall return to his family.
>
> —Leviticus 25:10

For example, if a widow had to sell her husband's land in order to survive, in the jubilee the land was to be restored to the family. At that time, also, the indentured servant was to be freed. The children of Israel were not to enslave one another, because, says Yahweh, "They are my servants, whom I brought forth out of the land of Egypt" (Leviticus 25:42). The jubilee year was a way of restoring the balance, of re-establishing the Lord's sabbath. It was even a renewal of creation when all people were given a right to their share of the land.

The prophets spoke of shalom as doing justice in the sight of the Lord. The false prophets proclaimed an easy peace with victory at the expense of the people because that was what the king wanted to hear (Jeremiah 6:14). But the true prophets' messages for the most part were not received in their own lifetime. Often they were punished for speaking what the rulers did not want to hear. Amos, for example, was not popular for speaking out against the injustices of the rich against the poor.

Decentralized Power

If we understand shalom in the broad sense of keeping the covenant with God, we then see that the work of the prophets in history was to call the people of Israel back to that responsibility as often as they lapsed. The whole of the prophetic writings tell the story of Israel's failures and attempts at renewing the covenant only to be followed by more serious failures on the part of its rulers. The people gradually put more and more trust in the king as the bearer of righteousness and shalom. The person of King David was thought for awhile to be the means of shalom. In contrast to expecting shalom through the king, the prophets tended to emphasize the earlier covenant of Moses. They called on the whole people to take up responsibility and power again and not to let their rulers speak for them, because the rulers did not speak well in the sight of the Lord. (See Hosea 10:3ff; 13:9–11.) In modern terms the king represented a centralization of power that made the people relatively powerless. Moses and the prophets, on the other hand, emphasized a democratic form of power in which the people took more of the responsibility for the community.

Keeping the Covenant

If shalom is understood to be the result of keeping the covenant with God, then it is because of their faithfulness that the prophets, such as Amos and Micah, spoke out against rulers both political and ecclesiastical as bearers of shalom. After the fall of Israel and Judah and the exile in Babylon, there was a breakdown of hope in earthly shalom. As a result, Israel became more and more pessimistic about the world in which it found itself. The hope of shalom was no longer in the nation as governed through its rulers, but rather in the exiled remnant, the faithful few. The hope of this remnant was shifted to the future and was not often described in historical or political terms. Instead, the later prophets spoke of the victory of God in cosmic, otherworldly, or apocalyptic terms, and used the image of the apocalyptic kingdom of God rather than "shalom" to express their hope in the future. The old language of God's action in history had become questionable. The faith of the followers of the ancient traditions was as strong as ever, but it took on new language and new symbols because the experience had changed. When history and the sacred institutions of kingship and priesthood no longer seemed to speak authoritatively and exclusively for God, hope for shalom by keeping the covenant had to be reformulated.

New Testament Concepts

In the New Testament, Jesus used this otherworldly, apocalyptic tradition as a means of calling people to faithful action in this world, especially when he preached of the kingdom of God. But the tendency throughout early Christianity was to move toward an otherworldly hope in place of hope in this world. This is a part of shalom. The part of shalom we will stress in this book, however, is more worldly and it is decentralized, because the covenant was made primarily with all the *people* at Mt. Sinai as opposed to the king, the ruler-person who was supposed to transfer shalom to the people. The notion of a dynasty of kings as a continuation of the person of David was expected to bring shalom. But by contrast, shalom through the covenant of Moses is more dynamic. The covenant included the necessity for all the people to keep the law, and the freedom for continual retelling and reinterpreting of the story of the acts of God in the light of new experiences and of different needs. We are also retelling the story of God's liberation to shalom. The retelling in this book calls for re-examination of our communities in light of shalom and asks each of us, "What would you like to do if you had the choice?" "How does your work community, your family community, your sexual identity, your civil community help you, free you, to choose?" "Are your communities run by 'kings' who make your choices and set your goals for you, or do they liberate you to make covenants with other free people before God?"

The absence of conflict, however, does not necessarily mean the presence of shalom. It may merely indicate that the needs of the individual or community have been submerged. We must fear the false harmony, the false peace, that suppresses the rights of others and represses their legitimate anger.

A *shalom* community is a body of people who have a peace based on a common vision, and a covenant with God that is given directly to the people and that is shared equally among them. Dynasties of leaders or kingdoms are powerless in this vision. People take charge of their own lives. They make their own decisions and answer directly to the covenant with God. At the same time they live at peace with others, for there is abundant life for all and liberation for the oppressed. This is the promised land of shalom that the Lord will give us even though we are still far away from it.

Shalom community includes people in all their richness and variety, as well as in their contrariness and need. Jesus intended that the good news be spoken to all the peoples of the earth. In some sense, our church communities as signs of shalom must represent this variety by including rich and poor, Black and white, Italian, Spanish, Asian, African people.

There are even now glimpses of this promised land, the vision of the shalom community. We continue to work at it in our one-hour-a-week vision of shalom—the church's celebration. We will now detail this vision and lay out a path for getting there.

CHAPTER 1
COMMUNITY IN THE CHURCH

We have glimpses of a world of peace and justice. In fact, in the church we deliberately arrange opportunities for experiencing our vision of shalom at least once a week. Even though it is only a rehearsal, a brief and sometimes otherworldly glimpse of shalom, worship services help us declare our intentions, our hopes, and our dreads as well as help us to listen to the word of God, which proclaims God's promise of shalom.

The vision of shalom is proclaimed in ritual celebration. Indeed, the sabbath day was first seen in the Bible as the shalom day when people stopped their toil and symbolically returned to Eden before the fall and before the curse of work and alienation from the soil, from the animal kingdom, from God, and from other humans. Thus, on the shalom day no working of the land or of animals was to be done. It was the day of rest from antishalom. Once a week we rest from our often fierce daily warrings at work and against other people. We reset our goals and visions on the sabbath. This one-hour-of-shalom takes place during the church's worship. Here we celebrate the rule of God when none shall be afraid. We celebrate the future vision of shalom.

THE MEANING OF CELEBRATION

A Christian service of worship is a performance of symbolic acts that lift up those visions and values which bind the community together. They are communicated primarily in an aesthetic (feeling) mode that expresses and invokes the spirit that unites the community by giving life to the community's values. In celebration we both protest and give thanks for the given conditions of the world.

Celebration in general is any of the ways (prayers, poems, parties, pilgrimages, feasts, fairs, fasts, music, or marches) by which a group of people act out or speak out the values that unite them. Services of worship are *deliberate* acts of symbolization using some prearranged form. A community cannot exist without celebration.

Celebration: Automatic and Essential

Communities of people will automatically find ways to symbolize their uniting values, although they may not call such behavior celebration or worship. They simply may have a party to honor a birth, an anniversary, a homecoming, a victory rally, a marriage, a new job, or the end or beginning of a new venture. If this does not happen within a collection of people, then the collection of people is not a community. Furthermore, if persons in the group do not participate emotionally in the symbolizing ceremonies, then there is a breakdown of community. Without the involvement of feelings, participants do not share in the community. To reverse an old slogan, "The people who stay together, pray together." In the case of religious celebration the shared values are, of course, God and the things that refer to God's shalom.

By comparison with a meeting to learn something (say a lecture series) or a meeting to do something (a political caucus), worship services concentrate on feelings, rather than on mental communication, or on the willingness to act. Music, dance, poetry, as well as dialogue, express the desire for union with God and with one another across all walls and boundaries. Shalom can be symbolically painted, sung, danced, or simply allowed to flow into the depth of our being in silent prayer.

Celebration: Protest and Thanksgiving

Just as a protest celebration can be the first step in a political act before political power comes into play, worship services can be the first step in a political act because they are a groaning of the spirit in us against the "travail" of bondage (Romans 8:21–27). They are groans of hope for a new world. Such "groans," as the apostle Paul calls them, are acts indicating that our spirits are not dead; they have not adapted to the present conditions of the world. They are still raging against dividing walls of hostility. These groans are often translated into public demonstrations, vigils, boycotts, strikes, petitioning of grievances, and other witness of protests. These groans of the spirit are even present in the child's prayer, "Rain rain go away—come again some other day." They are expressed in the act of peace demonstrators trying to levitate the Pentagon or casting out demons from an armament factory, or obstructing induction centers or troop trains, or fasting in jail. These acts are without political power themselves, but they evoke spiritual power. And as long as we have the spirit to protest present conditions rather than to adjust to them, we are still alive and spiritually powerful. When, for example, Rosa Parks refused to move to the back of the bus in Montgomery, Alabama, she was politically powerless. But her symbolic act was the first step toward civil rights for Blacks. The spirit of Blacks was ignited and it "groaned in travail," echoing her cry that "My feet are tired but my soul is at rest," as Blacks boycotted the buses by walking to work. This groan is the basic ingredient of symbolic acts. In order actually to change the conditions, symbolic acts require additional political organization through which the political power is tilted in favor of a change. Thus, worship can be the first step in political action. It is the protest against the present and also the hoping "for what we do not see" (Romans 8:25) . . . yet.

Worship services also can be the last step in a political act. Here we give thanks for the way things are. We not only accept the present conditions; we say we like them. We tell God and anyone who will listen: "I love my husband; I have for fifty years" (anniversary celebration); "I am glad Peggy was born" (birthday celebration); "Thank you, for her life. I accept her death" (funeral service); "God bless America" (Fourth of July ceremony); "Bill was a loyal employee" (retirement party). Besides hoping and protesting for change, we also have faith and gratitude for things as they are, and we perform symbolic acts in order to translate the feelings to our community. In so doing we reunite (bring shalom to) that community.

Every community must celebrate its victories (in thanksgiving and praise) and celebrate its defeats (in groans, lamentation, and repentance) or it will cease being a community. Celebration of victories gives a community its unity. Celebration of defeats gives it resolve. Both must be marked symbolically. Both life and death, the good and the bad, must be symbolized in community ritual because ritual, worship, and celebration are the language of the spirit. The only unforgivable sin, according to Jesus, is against the Holy Spirit (Luke 12:10). Loss of spirit is even more important than life and death. Without spirit our souls die, either personally or communally. This is why celebration is so central to a community. Spirit is finally the only reality that holds a community together. Our once-a-week celebration of shalom reconfirms things unseen—in this case our vision of the reign of peace, harmony, and justice. This hour of shalom when we live out our vision both expresses our limited hopes and invokes a greater vision of shalom.

Celebration: Being Reconciled or Inspired First

FIRST, BE RECONCILED

This brings us to the next set of ingredients crucial to Christian worship. Worship both expresses and invokes the right spirit, namely the spirit of reconciliation that brings a community together in shalom. If members of the community are not able to express a spirit of reconciliation in a just and peaceful community, there is no real community. This is illustrated in the life of Camilo Torres, a Catholic priest. A member of the Colombian upper class in Latin America, Torres decided to become a priest in order to serve the people. His sociological training was done in Europe, and as he studied he came to realize what he had not really known before: the incredible inequality between the wealthy few who lived well and the masses of poor peasants whose lives were spent in poverty, hunger, and disease. During Torres' youth, Colombia had experienced *la violencia,* a time of rioting and civil war that continued for ten years, when a previous leader of a third party had been killed. Camilo, like other Latin American intellectuals, identified the real, though covert, violence as that of the privileged few against the many. He saw violence as the hunger of a people who had a low per capita income ($300 per year) in Colombia, and as the structures of education, housing, politics and religion that oppressed the poor. He discovered beneath the obvious violence in the streets that the social structure itself was basically a violent one.[1]

When Camilo returned to Colombia from Louvain University in Belgium, he began teaching sociology at the National University in Bogotá as a way of making others aware and of doing something about the situation. After two years, it became clear to him that he could not operate as a university teacher. He became increasingly involved in politics. A chaplain to the students, he participated in a strike at the National University. Feeling that he had to do more, he decided to work for the masses of marginal poor people, focusing on their problems of inadequate health care, insufficient food production, and poor education. He soon ran into an obvious difficulty. A cleric is not supposed to become involved in politics. Torres' bishop questioned his concern with political action and made it clear that the young priest should leave either politics or the priesthood. The challenge was a difficult one. Although there were no models to guide his action, two statements of Jesus led him to make the choice that he made.

The first statement was: "You shall love your neighbor as

yourself" (Mark 12:31a). The supreme work of the Christian is love, thought Torres, and love means an effective caring for the needs of brothers and sisters. To remain a priest under the strictures that were placed on him would mean leaving these people in the same conditions and would be to abdicate his own power of loving.

A second statement of Jesus also helped him make his decision. Jesus said (and Camilo felt that it was addressed to him in a personal way): "If you are offering your gift at the altar, and there remember that your brother has something against you, leave your gift there before the altar and go; first be reconciled to your brother, and then come and offer your gift" (Matthew 5:23–24). For Camilo, these words meant that first he must work to improve the peasant's situation, not so much by charitable gifts, but by creating a new situation where the peasant could be self-supporting and self-respecting, and could share in the opportunities and possibilities of the country.

After much prayer and agony, Camilo decided to leave the priesthood in the consciousness that the eucharist, the sacrament of reconciliation and of sharing, could be celebrated only on the other side of the struggle. He decided to leave the altar (priesthood) in order to be reconciled to his brothers and sisters. To love his neighbors by creating a new situation free of hunger, poverty, and disease was a massive undertaking that took more than merely treating the symptoms with charity. Rather, the conditions that made them hungry and impoverished in the first place had to be changed. Changing the conditions would require changing the political and economic systems that benefited from these present arrangements. To do this, new political alternatives had to be introduced. However, as it happened, starting a new political party was impossible within the rigid arrangements that the Conservative and Liberal ruling classes had made among themselves. Politics in Colombia was a closed business. An even harder decision had to be made. What means were left for him to fulfill his call to help the people? He finally decided to join the guerilla fighters, to work underground with the people. After several months, however, he was ambushed by government forces and shot. His body was removed, and to this day even his mother does not know where he is buried. Presumably the government feared that he would be venerated as a martyr by the people who loved and revered their "Padre Camilo." [2]

Whether his choice was correct or not (some Christians think it was not), Camilo did in fact become an heroic symbol for many different Latin-American groups working for freedom and political representation for the people. Other Christian actions may be very different from his, but Camilo's struggle itself points out the power of his life as a symbol of sacrificial martyrdom. His own struggle has helped inspire other Christians in Latin America to gather together to continue the struggle for justice and for liberation.

What would it mean for us if we took as seriously as Torres did Jesus' message to be reconciled first before we returned to the altar? What would we do to change the conditions of poverty and hunger before we returned to a worship service? How would we reconcile ourselves to the wretched of the earth before we took communion again? Would we risk jail and death, position or money to find this reconciliation?

Christians will answer this choice differently. Certainly few will choose the way of Torres. But whatever way is chosen to fulfill Jesus' conditions for return to the altar, worship will never be the same for the person who risks jail, death, or anything he or she values highly. At times of great risk (of high honors, and great causes) prayer, worship, song, and dramatic acts come alive and captivate the human spirit. We automatically shout blessings (or curses) when we risk something—when life and death are at stake.

If our worship services in church are flat and dull, perhaps it is because our lives are flat and dull. Perhaps we are not living out the high deeds and honorable acts that evoke great compassion and self-respect. Therefore, our celebrations have little to celebrate. The Holy Spirit has to have some soul to work with before celebration can come alive. When we are working for shalom, when we are truly serving the neighbor where he or she hurts, then we return to the altar seeking and getting the nourishment required to keep going.

Celebration is real and strong when action is real and strong, when people are doing in reality what they are talking about in worship. Camilo Torres' living of Jesus' words made his life and his worship the same thing. Worship and celebration call us to love Jesus, to *do* his mission of liberation, and not merely to recite the words, "Lord, Lord" (Luke 6:46). Instead of once-a-week shalom, worship becomes more of the same, survival without a vision of shalom. Unless the action is there, coming to worship services is like stumbling into the wrong party. You are at best a spectator listening to someone else's mumbo jumbo.

INVOKE THE SPIRIT

However, there is another side to the picture. Sometimes this mumbo jumbo in worship catches on even if we come to the altar all wiped out and unreconciled. That is why celebration expresses the spirit of reconciliation (shalom), as in Torres' life, and also invokes the spirit to come back when we have lost it. It works both ways. Like grace, the spirit is given without being earned, but it also has to be taken. We are justified through faith, but faith without works is dead. We celebrate the small glimpses of shalom now, but we also project a future vision of shalom that we want God to help us bring.

People can have a personal sense of deadness and numbness at certain stages of their lives. This numbness may have something to do with the deadening nature of work or the tension of never being able to finish work. It may have to do with a sense of discouragement and weariness with work that stretches on indefinitely and that does not lead to anything worthwhile. For some it comes when they realize that even the work that they have chosen, because they thought it could contribute something to society, is also a dead end and makes as little difference as any other kind of work. Sometimes people get so depressed that life does not seem to mean anything. Men report this feeling in middle age. It comes when they realize that they have gone as far up on the ladder of advancement as they can or that their work has really not made an important difference after all. For women it can come when they realize that the children have grown up, and that they are alone and unloved because their husbands are too busy for them. Or it can happen when they realize that they have met everyone's needs but their own. Depression can also strike between two people in love, giving a sense of staleness even in a very good and enduring relationship.

In the long-range view, we discover that there are rhythms in human life that we have almost lost in our subjection to other people's decisions that rule our lives. The times of darkness, of inner numbness and weariness, are often fallow times, times when the earth of our being waits for a new time of creativity.

In biblical language, we experience ourselves to be part of the old world that is passing away, while at the same time we are part of the new. We have lost hope in the old, yet do not clearly see our way ahead into the new creation. We are spiritually perishing for lack of vision.

The new creation is Jesus' invitation to explore and to create new possibilities as a community of free people, an invitation to leave behind old ways of doing things that prevent people from growing. It means that we must cast off our old skins that limit our growth, break out into a new world, and create new forms and new institutions. It means following a vision of a new world of peace and justice, shalom.

The new creation is liberation, a process of taking up this vision. It is something offered to us, but it is also something we work at. Liberation is not real until the possibility of freedom is open to everyone, especially, as Jesus says, to "the least of these" (Matthew 25:40).

This vision of the future that theologians of liberation describe is a utopian vision. Utopia is a vision of the future that may not be practical. But as people are drawn to it, the vision begins to change them. Far from being impractical, Lewis Mumford says: "It is our utopias that make the world tolerable to us: the cities and mansions that people dream of are these in which they finally live."[3] Harvey Cox sees fantasy as central to worship, saying that creative fantasy can come only from people who are not too comfortable in the world.

Utopias, visions, dreams, fantasy life are gifts of the Spirit. They are the best medicine for depression. The vision we are invoking in this book is a vision of shalom. The church's service of worship is meant to be a one-hour utopia, where peace and justice (shalom) rule at least for a while. It is a model of what Christians think the world should be all the time.

If we do not have the hope lived out symbolically every seven days in church, we have to invent it by other kinds of celebration, if only in our private fantasies. Worship is both a protest that we do not have shalom yet and a thanksgiving for the few signs of shalom we do have. The vision of shalom is an ideal we invoke because we don't have it, but it is also a gift we bring to the altar because we are working for it. As Camilo Torres said:

> Like Christ, the Christian must become incarnate in humanity, and in its history and culture. Accordingly, he must forever seek the application of his life of supernatural love in the economic and social structures in which he should always be active.[4]

PLANNING WORSHIP

How can we make our church celebrations more inspiring, more in tune with shalom and with our spontaneous celebrations? How can they become re-creative and refreshing glimpses of shalom? In order for them to be re-creative, we must be creative. In order for them to be refreshing, we must bring fresh feelings to them and plan them to be fitting (fit for our feelings) ceremonies. Participation of the whole community is crucial.

A Whole Community Creation

A church can begin by asking various groups within the church to be responsible for different worship experiences during the year. Each group can work with the pastor to insure that something vital to the lives of its members is celebrated.

It is good to plan for worship in a private home and to worship when the group itself meets. Begin with a group of people, between ten and twenty in number. Remember that we should work at informality and help one another be relaxed and open. Most people are stiff toward and fearful of church ceremonies. Try out the stages of the service outlined below as an informal rehearsal for the service being planned. Include a reading or two from the Scriptures and a reading or two from a newspaper or journal. Give some time to open dialogue on the issues. In an atmosphere of receptive listening and of active discussion, people may find themselves relating to one another as they have not related before. The dialogue could flow into a discussion of concrete plans for the church celebration.

Ask yourselves: What kind of world do we want? What would shalom be like if we could bring it off? Then plan to create that vision for one hour. Look up scripture passages that deal with a theme that describes shalom to the group. Use works from contemporary writers together with the Scriptures. Use also the things in the worship that express creativity in our own lives. Celebrate the things people have made. Use them to decorate the place of worship. Let the offering be something into which people have put themselves. The man who has begun to cook can make a loaf of bread; a family could contribute homemade wine for the communion. A group of teenagers can dance or mime a scene from the Gospels, as in the play *Godspell*. Another group can present a song or a poem they themselves have composed.

The blessing of the bread and wine can be accomplished by a recitation of the New Testament or Old Testament formula by all the people (Mark 14:22–24; 1 Corinthians 11:23b–25; Exodus 12:8–14). The passage in Exodus is specifically a celebration of liberation and provides a fresh understanding of the traditional words for communion. Remind one another that as we drink the same "blood," we become blood brothers and sisters. Blood vengeance is over, we have broken the "wall of hostility."

If at the end the kiss of peace leads into dancing and a party, so much the better. What is most important in such a celebration is the breaking down of old barriers that separate us. Move worship out of the church building, and worship becomes an experience that is part of everyday life and that gives a whole new dimension to our homes, our friendships, and our actions. Such a worship service, especially where the people themselves initiate it without having to be led by someone in a formal leadership role, can be a graphic representation of the fact that we are all responsible for our shalom covenant with God.

Larger celebrations can be held in a lavishly decorated parish hall. Experiment with dance and song in forms that are meaningful to at least some of the people who are celebrating. Celebrations can be in a garden, in a park, or even as part of a block party—any place that is important because of the sense of community that has been formed.

When the location is moved from the sanctuary, we get new insights about how best to use the sanctuary itself. Some of the spontaneity occasioned by the new setting can then be brought back to the Sunday service in the church building.

Many people are designing their own worship services for their weddings. The service may dramatize the fact that the couple minister the sacred sign of marriage to each other. Many of these services are held outdoors or in a college or seminary lounge. Readings and music underscore the element of celebration, which the couple provides for relatives and friends. Some friends may play music, while others dance. If everyone contributes something to the occasion, the marriage becomes a time of joyous celebration. Wedding gifts can be simple creations that express something personal to the couple.

If different groups take the responsibility for worship presented for the whole group, it can be a way of bridging by experience the generation gap. Young people putting on a liturgy can work out how their parents may participate in it meaningfully. Older people setting up a celebration can tell the story of it in such a way that the younger people will understand its meaning. In this way the older people and the older form of services in the church would not be lost. A real sense of variety can be developed in our services.

Basic Elements of Celebration

1. INVITATION

The people are invited ahead of time if the celebration is to be somewhere other than the church. At the beginning of the celebration, the invitation is made clear once more. In essence, this is the "Call to Worship," but expressed more informally, calling forth a free response.

2. THE WORD OF PRAISE TO GOD

The people of the Lord live by challenge, and in their celebration they are challenged again by the vision of shalom when the hungry are fed and the oppressed are liberated. They hear the vision of shalom and realize how far away they are from it. This word is a call to renew their lives. They listen, meditate silently, have a dialogue together about the meaning of the message as good news, and explore ways of acting on it, to make real the vision in the world.

3. CONFESSION

It is a time of self-criticism when we allow God's word to touch our own lives. In traditional terms, it is the recognition of how we have fallen short, a plea for pardon, and a prayer for strength and love to live toward the vision.

If we acknowledge guilt, we should do something about it. Recognition without action results in a feeling of guilt, leads to bad faith, and is destructive to ourselves and to our relationships. The experience of guilt needs to be worked through and worked out. The responsibility is taken and a firm commitment made. If, for example, the American people as a whole are guilty of causing suffering in Vietnam, each of us needs to decide his or her own position with respect to this guilt. We are not simply guilty; we *can* act to liberate and to redeem. The how may not be clear, but we do not need to be immobilized by guilt, or self-satisfied because we are "sensitive" enough to feel guilty.

4. THE PARDON

The assurance of pardon is not a ritual that permits us to go back to business as usual. It affirms the forgiveness that enables us to confess our guilt and frees us to act in ways that reflect our repentance. Celebration is meant to result in action. The community may decide on some specific way in which the whole group or smaller groups can act on the basis of what they have understood has to be changed.

5. THE GOOD NEWS IS PROCLAIMED

The good news is given to us as a word that is *active,* that goes out and makes all things new, that changes everything. To the extent this does not happen, we are mouthing words we don't understand or we are deliberate hypocrites. *The good news is not freeing or liberating unless and until people really become free.* If Christians become free at the expense of others, then we have reason to question their devotion to the God of the Old and New Testaments, because this God is concerned about all people, especially about the poor.

Freedom is not purely spiritual. Unfortunately, we have overspiritualized freedom. In the Old Testament, freedom is highly visible in the Exodus out of Egypt and in the return from the Exile. In the New Testament, again it is highly visible in the outpouring of the Spirit and in the formation of a community where Jew and Gentile, slave and free, male and female met together as equals. Freedom in the community is the visibility of the good news, and it is this visibility that makes the difference. The Scriptures are read at this point in the service. The word is interpreted for today through a sermon or other media. People proclaim the modern-day good news in creeds and symbolic deeds, which communicate that God is in charge and that we are determined to know and act his will for shalom.

6. WE DEDICATE OURSELVES TO DO THE WORD

Up to now in worship we have gotten our faith in order by words. People usually stop here. Now we must decide what to *do.* In the letter of James, a great deal is said about the active visibility of Christians. "Faith apart from works is dead" (James 2:26). Martin Luther undervalued this little letter and insisted that people are justified through faith without works. Luther thought that James' insistence on the necessity that faith be fulfilled in action was corrupted by all of the abuses of "good works" in the medieval church. But perhaps we are in a different place and time today than Christians were during the Reformation. James told his hearers to be *doers of the word,* and not hearers only (James 1:22). Our action as Christians is to reflect the fact that God has elected the poor and the oppressed. We are to make distinctions that are biased toward the poor. James goes on and presses his case against us.

> What does it profit, my brethren, if a man says he has faith but has not works? Can his faith save him? If a brother or sister is ill-clad and in lack of daily food, and one of you says to them, "Go in peace, be warmed and filled," without giving them the things needed for the body, what does it profit?
>
> —James 2:14–16

Peace—that is, shalom—requires providing for the body, not just the spirit. In the words of an old Jewish proverb, "Love is sweet, tastes best with bread."

In Jesus' story of the last judgment, the condition of being chosen for eternal life was not correct faith. It was rather, "As you did it to one of the least of these . . . you did it to me" (Matthew 25:40). In this part of the service we commit ourselves, our money, and our resolve to a world of shalom.

7. SHARING AND COMMUNION

Communion takes on many meanings. It is a way of making future action and future reconciliation present in promise. Communion is also a celebration of Jesus in our midst and a celebration of our being made into a shalom community. It is a celebration of our struggle to be a community against all the walls of hostility that we meet in the process.

The root meaning of eucharist is thanksgiving for the gift of Jesus, who is our shalom. In the eucharist Jesus gives us the wholeness of his body and makes us one body. In the eucharist he does what he has announced. In the Old Testament, where hospitality was a sacred duty, sharing the meal was a sign of brotherhood (if not yet sisterhood). In the New Testament the meal signified the future messianic banquet, the second coming of the Son of man (and woman), when all the peoples of the earth would sit down together as equals.

When we share in the eucharist, we celebrate both our halting efforts at reconciliation and our hopes for the fulfillment of shalom. Like Camilo Torres, we too must test ourselves as we come to the altar, that we come in the honesty of real effort to overcome oppression, both our own and others'. For the eucharist represents the blood of Jesus—not only the blood of the sacrificial lamb, but the lifeblood of the struggle for justice and for peace.

8. THE KISS OF PEACE

The kiss of peace is becoming increasingly important in the new liturgies. In older services, people came in separately, listened to a predominantly verbal service, sang a few hymns, listened to a more or less professional choir, then left and shook hands with the pastor in a formal way. Today many people feel the need to express the sense of shalom and of community by the kiss of peace. For the people you know well, your friends, it may mean a warm handshake and the word "Peace." For those whom you do not know, it is an introduction, to say who you are, a handshake, and "I'm glad you're here," and thus a welcome. For those whom you love, it can be a warm hug. If this sign is given after the communion, it can be a way of interacting with one another, a way of continuing the promise of shalom beyond the service. If it is given before the communion, it may be understood as an effort to be reconciled to one another, to deal with the struggles that we all have.

Themes of Celebration

SEASONS OF SHALOM

In the Old Testament, the times of celebration not only include the weekly hour of shalom, but they also correspond to the rhythm of the seasonal celebrations. The Exodus is celebrated in the spring by the feast of Passover, and the feast of Tabernacles commemorates harvesting. Life has its rhythms, a balance between work and freedom from work, a time of worship and of dancing. In the New Testament, Sunday is the day of the resurrection, a day of new life and of re-creation. It is a new time, a time of the outpouring of the Spirit.

The year also brings a sense of great moments celebrated yearly. Easter commemorates not only resurrection but the zest of spring, whereas Thanksgiving is our harvest festival.

For many Christians, religious symbols have become difficult to talk about. They find themselves more in tune with secular forms of communication and celebration. In large part, this may be because all of us have attended too many noncelebrations. The words have lost their meanings, and, for many, celebration becomes almost impossible. This is partly because they were never understood as vital ingredients in everyone's yearly cycles of life or as rites of passage through one's life. The church seasons came to be established in cycles similar to the elements of the worship pattern: calling in to prepare for the Word of God (Advent, Lent); the proclamation of Christ's coming and overcoming death (Christmas and Easter); and the dedication to strive for shalom (Epiphany, Pentecost). Like the worship pattern, one gets ready, receives the Word, and goes out to do the Word.

LIFE CYCLES

The church has also celebrated in its rites the life cycles of people from birth to death. Birth (in baptism) is followed by puberty (first communion and/or confirmation), vocational choice and commitment (ordination or commissioning), marriage (rite of matrimony), and death (unction or funeral service). Two other rites are more general. They are confession of guilt (confessional) and fulfillment (eucharist). These rites constitute seven sacraments in the Roman Catholic Church. Although Protestants have only two sacraments, all of these stages in a person's life are celebrated in one way or another. If we do not observe them (birth, marriage, death), then the spiritual realities haunt us and even torment us.

These themes of celebration are the essential ones, but there are many others that arise in daily life, such as moving to a new house, starting school, ending a war, burning a mortgage, getting legislation passed, and stopping the building of an unneeded highway.

PUBLIC THEMES

Normally the church has been restricted to the private realm of seasonal and life cycles while the public problems of this world—peace, justice, liberation—were often ignored as political rather than otherworldly spiritual matters. I reject this restriction because the shalom theme is a vision of abundance, liberation and peace in *this world.* These public themes must be reclaimed and celebrated as well as the private seasonal and life cycle themes. Both are themes in our vision of shalom.

Although we have a glimpse of shalom in our worship, it is still a vision far off in the future. I believe we live in a time when economic inequality, misuse of technology in warfare, abuse of the environment, and exploitation of women and Third World peoples cry out for public, not private, solutions. We know how to encourage private accumulation of wealth (through tax incentives and guarantees of profit), but we have not yet learned how to encourage communities to solve their problems.

Our churches may be a good starting point for the rebuilding of community. There, small communities can begin to rediscover the vision of shalom and to challenge the larger church and society with workable methods of making society more just. Today these small communities can exist comfortably in the shadow of the churches and on the margins of other social institutions. They will be "Exodus communities," working for liberation, aware that liberation is both private and public. They will be communities both of retreat and of action, sensitive to the needs and rhythms of human life.

These communities may be Pentecostal groups with a real concern for brotherhood and sisterhood. They may be groups of ecumenical Christians gathered for social action. They may be anonymous Christians—people of good will who would not directly identify themselves as Christians and yet through whom God speaks to us once again.

SOME EXAMPLES OF EXODUS COMMUNITIES

Some groups have developed house churches—small groups that meet together once or twice a month for study, action, and celebration. Some of these groups number as few as a dozen people. Their emphasis has not been only social action, though house churches have been linked with the peace movement.

University eucharistic communities often have such a double orientation of worship and social action. The group may be quite large, but within subgroups, the members can come to know one another intimately. In this case, the minister is a facilitator. These ministries are linked to formal church structures; yet they have a degree of freedom that is not available to the ordinary church group.

The Society of Priests for Free Ministry (SPFM, also known as the Fellowship of Christian Ministries) began in 1967 when concerned Catholic priests and laity started to question seriously the church's failure to respond to a broader range of pastoral needs made evident in the wake of Vatican II. This group has operated primarily on the periphery of the institutional church while remaining faithful to its spirit and early traditions. Originally founded to challenge mandatory celibacy, SPFM has continued to expand its horizon of alternative ministries by becoming involved in social as well as personal ministries, not the least of which is the celebration of worship, much in the style described above. Presently in the experimental stage is a certification program for women and nonordained Christians engaged in social ministry, and a pilot project with old people to develop a ministry of advocacy for sick people, for judicial reform, for corporate responsibility, and for other issues of concern.

Another model is the Congregation for Reconciliation in Dayton, Ohio. The group was originally set up as a training program for lay ministry, but is composed of people who are uncomfortable within the traditional parish setting. The church is committed as a group to social action in the city, and it has a number of projects to its credit. Their largest action has been the boycott of the Gulf Oil Corporation. This group is primarily composed of white, professional, middle-income people.

Originally the group was funded by the United Presbyterian Church. A year later the United Church of Christ agreed to sponsor the church. At the moment, one of the problems seems to be that people view their relationship to the parent churches in different ways. For some, the relationship to traditional theological and ecclesiastical forms is considerably stronger than for others.

The group is not only task-oriented but also community-oriented. There is talk of relationships as an extended family, with a good deal of sharing and common use of resources belonging to one or another of the members. Worship services are held twice a month and are planned and carried out by small groups of two or three.[5]

Women have also seen the need to form communities of reflection, action, and celebration. For them, many of the traditional religious symbols need drastic reinterpretation. In worship experiences, the she-ness of God needs to be expressed. Liturgies developed with this in mind not only express a hidden dimension of God, they also give women something to glory in.

One women's group reworded Mary's jubilant song, the Magnificat, as follows:

> My soul magnifies the Lord,
> and my spirit rejoices in God my Savior,
> For she has regarded the low estate of her handmaiden,
> For behold, henceforth all generations will call her blessed;
> for she who is mighty has done great things for me, and holy is
> her name.
> And her mercy is on those who fear her from generation to
> generation.
> She has shown strength in her arm,
> She has scattered the proud in the imagination of their hearts,
> She has put down the mighty from their thrones,
> and exalted those of low degree;
> She has filled the hungry with good things,
> and the rich she has sent empty away.
> She has helped her servant Israel,
> in remembrance of her mercy,
> as she spoke to our mothers,
> to Sarah and her posterity forever.[6]

Another group of women developed a meaningful worship experience based on a common meal that celebrated Eve and the apple. Whereas the original story was intended to put down Eve and women as temptresses, this group saw Eve as a generous, courageous woman, willing to take risks and to think big. The climax of the meal came with a common eating of the apple, and the meal itself took place with singing and laughter—a real experience of celebration and liberation.

CONCLUSION

There can be many celebrating communities, some within traditional church structures, some forming new patterns of community at the boundary. These communities can seek to pattern out a vision of shalom. In these communities, a life-style of caring and sharing, of creativity, can be begun in new ways and celebrated. Gifts of each person, often gifts that he/she did not know existed, are called forth, and new ministries take shape and are celebrated. These communities may well become the beginnings of shalom. One member of such a community wrote:

> If we are to be creators, we must begin to think in terms of a whole new work ethic. The reward will not be in higher wages, another rung on the ladder, the acclaim of our peers, but in creative forces which flow within us and accomplish in our own lives the gracious work of transformation.[7]

The harmony of our once-a-week shalom always faces a rude shock when reality sets in. We need, therefore, to work very hard and carefully on how we go about implementing our vision of shalom in the real world. We will look at a method next.

CHAPTER 2
A METHOD OF CREATING COMMUNITY

To accompany a vision of shalom, we need a method for reaching it. Paul named the process as breaking down the "wall of hostility" (Ephesians 2:14). Before we begin breaking any walls down, however, we need to spell out our method in detail. How do you get to the vision step by step? First of all, we will look at the basic requirement for community—communication. If there is no communication, there is no community. Second, we will examine the theological background that informs the concept of community. Third, we will describe a method used successfully in South America to overcome the wall of illiteracy there. Then we will spell out the stages of the process, which can be summarized as: (1) Naming, (2) Analyzing, (3) Envisioning, (4) Acting, (5) Reflecting, and (6) Following Through.

COMMUNITY REQUIRING COMMUNICATION

> I respond although I will be changed.[1]

> The living speech of a community results from the polarization of acts and thoughts; like the spark which crosses the dark gap between the positive and negative poles of electricity, speech is a flaming arc connecting different generations.[2]

In a sense, speech is community. People may work, share a physical place, and even engage in the common task of childbearing and childrearing, without communication. Until they can go beyond the ordinary everyday talk to share with one another needs and hopes, goals and disappointments, even very solid relationships miss an essential dimension. I begin to hear when I am able to take the risks of hearing others, of allowing myself to be changed. I begin to speak when I can take the risks of attempting something that may fail, that others will refuse to hear, or that they will gladly receive. Often I do not know that my words have enabled and empowered others to speak. If I have the courage to speak, others too can speak because they are no longer alone.

Where people dialogue with one another, they create community. With others we learn to say who we are, what we need, what others need, what we can do, in a group that affirms us. We also learn to listen to others when they say who they are and what they need. Dialogue is not only a matter of words back and forth, an endless stream of sound, but it is *interaction,* a speaking that calls forth a practical and active response from others. In speaking, in listening, in allowing ourselves to be changed through our response, we become community.

THE POWER OF THE WORD

The Hebrews had a concept of the word that was more than talk. The Divine Word was active and effective. It was the word that created the world and approved it (Genesis 1). It was a word spoken to establish a people and set them apart for the Lord in the giving of the commandments. That word was both a word of covenant and a word of formation (Exodus 34). The prophets speak the word of the Lord to restore the covenant relationship of shalom and to rebuild the community. That word is active, as the Lord says through the prophet Isaiah:

> So shall my word be that goes forth from my mouth;
> it shall not return to me empty,
> but it shall accomplish that which I purpose,
> and prosper in the thing for which I sent it.
>
> —Isaiah 55:11

The reverse is also true. God can be affected and changed by human words. God "repents" of anger when the people turn away from their sin in action (Jeremiah 18:8). In the story of Jonah, the Lord revokes the punishment of Nineveh when the people in response to the king's edict do penance and turn away from their sin (Jonah 3:1–10).

In the New Testament, the response to the Divine Word is also active. It is never a purely theoretical hearing, but always a doing. Jesus saw the relationship between speech and action as the relationship between a tree and its fruit (Luke 6:43–45). Also there is the figure of Jesus as the true vine, together with the disciples, his branches, who can bear fruit only if they abide in him (John 15:1–11). And in the early church, members of the body of Christ are described as "speaking the truth in love" (Ephesians 4:15). Above all, in Jesus, God is vulnerable and can be changed—affected by the human dialogue. Dialogue then is not a mere interchange of words; it is a form of interaction that has an effect on persons.

Dialogue means confrontation and conflict. The success of dialogue may not be whether all flows smoothly and evenly, but whether in fact it allows real differences to surface so that action may be taken. Struggle is part of the Old Testament. Jacob wrestles with the divine visitor and overcomes him in the early hours of the morning. As a result he is renamed "Israel" because he has struggled "with God and with men, and [has] prevailed" (Genesis 32:28). In his suffering the innocent Job challenges God under his time of trial (Job 31:5–40), and God vindicates the sufferer before his accusers, at the same time as he expands Job's vision (Job 42:7–17).

Not all talk is dialogue. Talk can also be empty chatter, a new way of avoiding the talk that we need to have, a way of keeping everything the same and on the surface. Chatter can be fear of silence, an unwillingness to speak our minds, or a positive refusal to deal with the other person seriously. However, there is also a kind of small talk that functions as a bridge where we learn to speak with one another of things at first less important and then more important.

Silence can be a way of not speaking when we need to speak. It may be an inability to speak out of a sense of powerlessness or a kind of discouragement. It is a way of not being there.

Power comes from speaking up. As powerless people learn to speak up, they discover the power that they really do have. As they speak together and develop common concerns, they develop communal power. Ordinary people have power when, through dialogue, they become a community. In Brazil, the work of Paulo Freire has in fact pointed up the feeling of power that people come to experience as they begin to speak, to read, to learn, to communicate together—to emerge from their culture of silence from behind the wall of illiteracy.

COMMUNICATION POWER IN BRAZIL

In Brazil, as in most of Latin America, illiteracy runs over 50 percent. The poorest section of Brazil, the rural northeast, is controlled by the local landowners.[3] In this part of the country, illiteracy is closer to 90 percent. The democratic process is nonexistent. Since literacy is a requirement for the vote, most of the peasants of the northeast are politically disfranchised. Even where they do have the vote, the plantation owner calls the tune. Either they vote for his man or they run the risk of his disfavor. In effect, the landowner is all-powerful and often has his own small army. He is the local government, the police, the source of work, and the local store. In many cases even the church is subject to his power.

But within this situation, the Catholic bishops began a radio literacy program in the 1950s. Soon many university students volunteered to assist. The program itself was designed by Paulo Freire, who had gained extensive experience of the people's powerlessness through his own work as an advocate for the people. Working with a liberal government department of education, he set up a program in which the participants learned to read and write in a period of six weeks. Some of them had been to schools as children for one or two years without learning to read and write, yet by using Freire's method they learned in a period of weeks. The method had such sensational results that by 1963–64 a broad crash program had been set up whereby it was anticipated that 20,000 "circles of culture" or study groups would reach some two million adults. Obviously the program had a political payoff for the liberal government, who hoped to gain a new constituency. In a country ruled by a wealthy elite, where the poor majority could not even vote, literacy training alone could drastically change the balance of political power simply through granting the right to vote.

Freire's work began to be successful on a grand scale. The populist elements of the government seemed to be getting too powerful, and as a result the military took over the government in 1964. One of the first acts of the new government was to put Freire himself in jail and to close down the literacy training program. After six months, Freire was exiled to Chile, where he began to try out his method under the Christian Democratic government there. Today he has set up an institute of cultural action with the World Council of Churches in Geneva, which functions as a training and research center in both literacy and political action.

What was so different about Freire's method? The real difference was that he saw reading and writing as communication, and not merely as skills divorced from the act of communicating something. As he looked at the reading books available to the peasants, he found them totally unrelated to any of their actual concerns. They were in fact not unlike the Dick and Jane readers some of us were raised on. In order to find out how the peasants spoke about themselves and their lives, he sent out teams of experts to *listen* to the people talk, to find out what bothered them, what they thought important, how they saw their world. He found that when people saw their own concerns in print and in pictures, they learned to read very quickly. Not only that, they gained a whole new sense of self-worth and of power.

When Freire went to Chile in 1965, he followed the same procedures. There the peasants described what happened to them as they learned to read and write. One said: "Before the agrarian reform [and literacy training] I didn't even think. Neither did my friends."[4] Others said: "Before we were blind, now the veil has fallen from our eyes." "I came only to learn how to sign my name. I never believed I would be able to read, too, at my age."[5] Whereas before, most Chileans lived in a culture of passivity and of silence, unable to understand their situation and feeling themselves to be powerless, today they experience themselves as people with power. Unfortunately, in Brazil the people's awakening was tragically cut off.

Why were these groups in Brazil and Chile so effective? In our society, learning to read is no great thing; it is simply a matter of going to school, more or less.

But in Latin America, reading and writing were crucial to some life and death concerns. Freire began with the actual concerns and problems that the peasants themselves articulated, problems of poverty, inadequate housing, unemployment, sickness, and impoverishment for their children.

Freire rejected the ordinary notion of literacy training and of education generally in what he called the "banking theory of education."[6] According to this theory, the teacher is a banker who makes regular deposits of knowledge in the minds of the students. The student works to memorize the information, so that he or she can give the correct answer on demand. If she or he can answer correctly, there are adequate funds in the account and the student has met the test. If not, the student fails. The years of education progressively build up knowledge assets so that after a specified period, the student is able to go out into the world, and live off the interest from the account.

This theory assumes two things that Freire rejects. It assumes, first, that knowledge, as a "deposit" or thing that can be handed on, manipulated and used, exists independently of the people who know. Secondly, the theory assumes that learners are passive. Not until the account is "full" does the learner become a knower. Human beings are thus seen more like reservoirs or conduits for knowledge. With this theory, there is always the concern that knowledge not be "watered down."

By contrast, Freire sees the learning process as a matter of dialogue. The learner is also a knower who has something to contribute actively, as well as being an active listener. Instead of a process that programs out the talents and experience of the learner, Freire sees the learning process as one that empowers people to understand and use the rich store of experience and knowledge they already have. The process then becomes one whereby a facilitator helps the learners-participants to question the actual situation in which they find themselves and the inevitability of that situation, to raise the possibility of alternatives, and to allow them actively to decide their own future.

Learners, however, always come out of a situation. In Freire's context, this situation is one of oppression. This situation requires that the learning process be one of liberation, made all the more difficult to the extent that the oppression is hidden and all-encompassing. Thus Freire points out, that the oppressed

> must acquire a critical awareness of oppression through the praxis of this struggle. One of the gravest obstacles to the achievement of liberation is that the oppressive reality absorbs those within it and thereby acts to suppress man's consciousness. Functionally, oppression is domesticating. To no longer be prey to its force, one must emerge from it and turn upon it. This can be done only by means of the praxis: reflection and action upon the world in order to transform it.[7]

For example, a coordinator or facilitator shows a slide or a picture of a local factory. Some men are lounging on a corner with nothing to do, and there is a sign posted, "No Work." Unemployment is the meaning of the picture, as it relates to the reality of the peasants' lives. Then the question *Why* is raised, which leads the discussion to the larger picture: the economic conditions of the country, the social structure, the inequality of the wealthy few and the many poor. The immediate personal situation of the peasant is thus understood to be related to the national, political, and structural problems. The next step, following questioning of experience in the context of political reality, is practical action, *praxis*. Without this stage, understanding is incomplete, and could be mere talk as described above. If learning results only in talk, then people are more apathetic and more discouraged than before. They ask, "What difference does it all make after all?" The practical question is always: "What is the difference?"

Freire begins with an emphasis on men and women as creators of their world, a world of work and of tools, a world of stories, of songs, of poetry, and of dance. This is an experience of surprise for the peasants, for they have always thought of themselves as unimportant and of no value. After going through some weeks of Freire's learning process, they discover themselves further as people with power over their economic life and community. They see themselves as political people. Freire himself, however, stops at this point. For him, the question of a change in consciousness, a change in cultural patterns, is more significant than actual political activism. At this point in Brazilian history, it in fact may be the only kind of change that is possible. The brakes have been placed even on this kind of change.

In the United States, although our situation is very different, the method of group action for change has also become increasingly important. Sensitivity groups reflect one form of such a process. The danger in such groups has been that the groups become imprisoned in themselves. In this country the Freire group perhaps would embody some of the best insights of sensitivity, but also would look out to the larger context of the world in which we live, to see personal and immediate problems in the context of the larger society. The process will develop a very different style for us who in many ways benefit from a system that also oppresses us as well as oppressing less fortunate people.

My own experience has been that the method can help us deal with our own sense of powerlessness. For us, it will not be a matter of learning how to read and write, but rather a matter of speaking out, of saying what needs to be said in spite of the consequences, and of learning to confront others. Speaking out is the basic condition of building our vision of shalom. Speaking out is required in all steps of the process that names, analyzes, envisions, acts, reflects and follows through in the course of breaking the walls of hostility.

STAGES OF THE PROCESS

Basically, the stages of the process are developed from Freire's own model, together with methods that have been developed in this country. The basic aim is to get people talking to one another with a new sort of freedom, to allow them to look at their world in a new way, to make some new decisions about their world, and to begin to change that world. This method is a way of learning to take power over our own personal lives and in our society, a way of connecting and reconnecting with other people. We are powerless in isolation. Together we can build a more humane style of life with one another, in confidence toward the future.

The stages of the process may vary, but generally they are in this order:

1. Naming the basic issues, concerns, problems.
2. Analyzing these issues so that they can be understood in their basic structure.
3. Envisioning a new future—allowing free play for creativity and imagination, breaking out of the present.
4. Acting—beginning with a doable action, then a series of doable actions, and, with experience, working up to strategies.
5. Reflecting on the significance of the action and evaluating the effectiveness of the process.
6. Following through.

Dialogue is the pattern throughout. Leaders and resource people are there not to increase their own power, but for the sake of the community. Let us look at these stages in more detail.

1. Naming the Basic Issues

A group begins by raising questions such as the following:

—In what areas of our lives are we active? In what areas are we passive?

—How would we like to develop our own powers? If we could choose freely, what sort of work would we like to do?

—What contradictions do we experience in our lives and in our world? Projecting those contradictions ahead ten years, what kind of a world will we have then? If I go on as I am now, what kind of a person will I be?

—What concrete problems would I like to work on, to make changes in? What areas would I like to see grow stronger?

—If things go on as they are now, what do I *fear* will happen? What do I *hope* the future will bring? How can I help create the desired future?

Some of the issues that groups work on are: work, marriage, community, personal integration, personal and social liberation as a woman or a man, and life-styles of caring and sharing. Still other issues are children's liberation, sexuality, family, jobs, economics, peace, ecology, and energy. Obviously, many of these concerns are interrelated. The following chapters of this book are resources for the discussion of such themes.

If the group is a large one, the group leader or facilitator may want to explain the process briefly and let people divide into small groups of perhaps three or four, so that each person can take his or her time to describe the issue that he or she would like to work at and how it affects his or her life. It may take thirty to forty minutes to name the issues.

All the small groups would then regather to list the issues they raised. Often the same issue will be described in different terms. The task then will be to combine those that seem to belong together. Recording these issues on newsprint is useful at this stage to get all the questions down so that everyone can see what is going on. The number of issues to be worked on will be divided by who wants to work on what. If the group is on a weekend retreat, some practical decisions have to be made to limit the choices. If it is an ongoing group, individuals will choose which concern is most important at a given moment, and work on another concern later.

2. Analyzing the Issues

At this stage, each individual describes or pictures her or his situation in more detail. The aim here is not to show how it is an issue, as in the first stage, but to see it clearly as a concern that is experienced in the lives of different people. Some general questions are the following:

—What are the contradictions in my situation?

—How do I experience my situation as oppressive? Do I oppress others? For example, how is my job oppressive for me? Do I, in fact, also make others in this situation less free? Or, again, are marriage and freedom contradictory?

—What values of our society am I comfortable with? What values am I uncomfortable with?

—How do my values differ from those of my parents? of my children?

Once the issues are clearly analyzed, not only in their personal reality but also in their social dimension, the group can determine what further information it needs. Often this can be obtained by the participants themselves. Too frequently, we expect "outside experts" to have all this information. Myles Horton, who has worked for many years with community people in Appalachia, describes a situation in which people themselves decided when and where to act to improve their conditions. In one area the people wanted to set up a newspaper to keep in touch with each other because they were geographically isolated. Myles Horton was asked to provide the resource people for a weekend meeting. Twenty or thirty community people came, and as they started talking to each other, they discovered that they were their own best resources. Talk was fast and furious, and somehow there was no time for the experts. What emerged was a people who discovered their own knowledge and their own power and ran with it.

Thomas Sanders, an American observer of the Freire method, put it this way:

> My own most memorable impression from visiting these classes [using the Freire method] is of the capacity of people of limited education for thoughtful analysis and logical articulation of the issues when the issues are linked to their everyday life.[8]

3. Envisioning a New Future

By this time, our problems, dissatisfactions, hostilities, and frustrations have been exposed. We are looking realistically at our lives, with some notion of things we would like to see different. But at this stage we should set aside these frustrations, the limitations and commitments of every day, and unleash our imagination. Allow it to fly free, to roam where it will. Make "I wish . . ." statements about your life, especially in the area of concern. "I would like . . ." or "I hope . . ." For example, "I would like to work three days a week and have some more time with my children," or "I wish I could travel," or "I wish I could walk down the streets at night without being afraid." What would you wish for yourself? For your spouse? For your children? For people you know? What would you wish for your neighborhood? For the people you don't know? What kind of a country is needed to make these wishes come true? What kind of a world? What is your vision of shalom? These wishes and visions can be listed and shared. But they can also be expressed creatively in free art, a wood carving, a photograph, a dance, a skit, a song, or a poem. Wishes do in fact come true sometimes. Our problem is that we seldom allow ourselves to envision a world of shalom. Instead, we settle for a world imposed on us by others. As free people, it is our task to name, analyze, and dream our own dreams and also actively to enter into the creation of a new world.

4. Acting

Some wishes imply conflict with others. A person whose idea of happiness is an all-white neighborhood will conflict not only with Black people who want to live in such a neighborhood but also with other white people who think that Black people should live in that neighborhood. Suppose a group takes as its theme "Building a City" (outlined later in this book), and begins to work on the question of neighborhood. Discussion will zero in on the issue of what makes a neighborhood worth living in, sameness or variety, and then go on to some ways of achieving that neighborhood.

The doable action initially may be to facilitate dialogue between white and Black people. Invite both groups to a discussion and hear what their wishes are about the city. Listen to one another as you discuss crime in the streets, poor schools, and deteriorating neighborhoods. Further doable actions might involve community action to prevent panic, to facilitate mutual understanding, or to open up the neighborhood to outsiders in such a way that they can participate.

Another group may plan action against the city's political machine to open up city politics to concerned citizens. Here the group will need a very careful analysis of the power structure as it actually exists in the city or town. At the same time, the analysis should reveal the weak points of the system. It is not monolithic and unconquerable, but as vulnerable as the people who make it up. Political machines are particularly vulnerable because they are not noted for incorruptibility. A little exposure, some community indignation and some citizens' pressure could make an enormous difference.[9] We are bound by the myth of powerlessness, which invests the political reality with an oversized power.[10]

The second myth for us in the arena of political action is not the fatalism of the Brazilian peasant, but the bias of false loyalty. We assume that leadership is benevolent at the same time that we cynically talk about dirty politics in general. We are made to think and we come to believe that working to change an institution, or even a small community, is being disloyal to it. To the extent that a society makes such criticism look like disloyalty and treachery, the society has ceased to be open; it has become a coercive society, whether it is a family, a commune, a company, a city, or a country.

Often, however, very positive action in our world can feel like reaction to what has been done. The terms of our action are already set, and we feel overwhelmed by the magnitude of the task of creating a new society. Yet Freire insists that this action nonetheless can be a "transformation of the world. And as praxis this action requires theory to illuminate it. Men's activity is theory and practice; it is reflection and action . . . directed at the structures to be transformed."[11] The importance of theory is the importance of the long-range vision and the long-range action. Short-range alternatives can very well leave the situation essentially unchanged or even worse than before, if people come to despair.

5. Reflecting

This is an essential part of the process and refers both to the process itself as well as to the action that flows out of it. Reporting it can include what you did, what happened as a result, how you felt about its success or failure, why you thought it went well or badly, and what can be done to follow that through. The point is to succeed even at a small action. If the action turned out not to be doable, then that, too, forms part of the evaluation. It may be doable only after some other things are done first.

The reflection stage is important for a number of reasons. In the first place, if something goes well, we tend to feel that we do not need the evaluation, just because it went well. But we need to know why it succeeded, whether it was just accidental or whether the dynamic was as we thought it was. In the second place, we tend to evaluate our failures much more strongly, to give them more weight, than our successes. We punish ourselves for our failures, but take our successes for granted. We should get the full mileage out of our successes, gain hope from them, come to a better sense of ourselves as actors, as people who do have the power to influence and change their world. It is important even to celebrate individual and group victories. Rejoice in them, savor them, celebrate them in worship and with parties.

In working with groups, we have often experienced a sense of depression emanating from the group itself. There are, I think, a number of factors that sometimes converge to the point at which the group is immobilized. In part, depression occurs when intelligent and sensitive people come together to analyze the problems of the large social structure. The analysis seems to show a structure much more powerful than we are, against which we are helpless. The real culprit is the talk itself, which does not take account of doable actions. Freire calls it "alienating blah-blah-blah." The temptation at this point is to give up, when in fact it is the moment to zero in on doable action and to work on strategy.

The doable action may not be necessarily the best possible action. To search for that hypothetical best would be to lock ourselves in again on the intellectual level, to spend precious time arguing, when we should be pulling together to act. It is precisely at this point that middle-income people short-circuit their own efforts to bring about change. Effectiveness comes about through concerted action, where it is clear that the group itself has ways of making decisions and can take initiative on the larger scene. Such a group does not need to become locked into any strategy; thus it has the tactical element of surprise. To become overcommitted to strategies is to lock ourselves in, to render ourselves powerless.

Within the group itself, leadership questions will emerge sooner or later. There is nothing wrong with "power plays" if they are made consciously, and if there is some method for *sharing* leadership. It may be that a strong leader gives the rest of the group something to test itself against—if the leader draws out the leadership of others. The crucial experience may be when the members of the group symbolically "kill the leader" and say, "We don't need you as leader anymore; come and join us as a participant." Not too many models exist for a group that has developed a style of effective action in which all the members participate in decision making. The problem easily can become one of sheer clumsiness when the smallest decision takes hours to make. A balance of strong leadership and full group participation must be sought constantly.

6. Following Through

A. SUPPORT GROUPS

Part of our experience of powerlessness is the result of the centralization of our institutions. Most of our institutions have gotten larger and larger. Businesses merge, government agencies add new services and new personnel, churches merge and centralize, and bureaucracies everywhere become more centralized. Even within the bureaucratic structure, let alone outside it, individuals feel more and more powerless.

If the real question is one of restoring power to people, we need to work at decentralizing. This may have certain costs, both financially and in efficiency, but the gains in terms of personal contribution and well-being and power will more than balance the cost. Support groups can help people adjust to this kind of decentralization within institutions, and can help to create nonbureaucratic ways of work and of service.

Support groups will probably operate most effectively if they are both within and outside the institution. If they are wholly within, they still leave the individual at the mercy of the institution; to be only outside may be to create an alternative life-style that has no effect on the institution.

This method should lead to the establishment of support communities that can serve as an ongoing forum for new ideas and personal strength. In such groups, people can listen, affirm, evaluate, and suggest alternatives, but they also can support individuals in the form of action taken. Such a group will function effectively to the extent that it is able to work out a generally accepted point of view. Otherwise the group will continually be at the stage of questioning basic assumptions without being able to go beyond that stage. The support group itself will probably not be basically task oriented; rather its members will belong to different task groups. Thus the support group will have a variety of inputs and will be able to deal with some of the personal needs of the members.[12]

B. THOUGHTS ON STRATEGY

(1) **Know the weak points of the system.** There are more than you think.

—Oversized institutions are unwieldy. Individuals do not hang together at times of stress.

—Bureaucratic structures can create resentments because structures are not human.

—Human nature is on your side because systems cannot contain it.

—Power elites have power, but they are never very unified.

(2) **Look for allies.** Within the system there are dissatisfied people as well as sensitive people who see its oppressiveness. Identify these people, because they can help. Take advantage of disagreements among elites. In the past, elites have used tactics of divide and conquer against the rest of us; we can use these tactics ourselves, at the same time as we attempt to gain the support of those who are sympathetic.

(3) **Know your own strong points, both as individuals and as a group.**

—Take initiative and refuse to be on the defensive. The defensive is a position of reaction, and the battleground is usually on your own territory.

—Don't fight every battle. Choose your battleground.

—Establish linkages with other groups. Too often activist groups get caught in the bind of competition or of an absolutist ideology. We need all the help we can get from one another, even though we may disagree on priorities.

(4) **Know your own weak points.**

—Moral rectitude doesn't replace knowing the situation in detail and as a whole.

—Our culture often creates in us the inability to live and work cooperatively. To begin to live as community is a long learning process for most of us who have been brought up as individualists. But we have political leverage only to the extent that we can work together, can submerge some differences in favor of common action.

CONCLUSION

The ideas that lie behind this book are themselves the result of a process, of my own experiences in using the above method with groups of people around the country.

This book is another stage in the dialogue. It is intended as part of an ongoing reflection/action process. It is not intended as a textbook or a source of information for "banking" education.

This chapter has outlined a process and the stages of a method that names our issues, analyzes them, envisions alternatives, acts to get them, reflects on that action, and follows up as we repeat the process.

The following chapters are intended to be an exploration of certain walls of hostility that prevent shalom community. What I have written may serve to start discussion, to illuminate personal experience, or to provide good discussion by vigorous disagreement.

Use the following chapters in any order that appeals to you or your group. The pattern is often circular and inclusive. Each theme requires some discussion of other themes. Talking about work structures will lead into family structures, sex roles, and insecurity in city and world. At the same time, those who perform the doable action will have to zero in on one or several specific areas, even though the group will be conscious of the implications of that change in other areas of life.

Let us begin now to apply our vision and method to five "walls of hostility" that must be broken down on the road to shalom. I believe the most all-pervasive wall is the one between women and men.

CHAPTER 3
SEX, SLAVERY, AND LIBERATION

In America the independence of woman is irrecoverably lost in the bonds of matrimony. If an unmarried woman is less constrained there than elsewhere, a wife is subjected to stricter obligations. . . . The Americans . . . require much abnegation on the part of women and a constant sacrifice of her pleasures to her duties, which is seldom demanded of her in Europe. . . . Nor have Americans ever supposed that one consequence of democratic principles is the subversion of marital power or the confusion of the natural authorities in families.

—Alexis de Tocqueville[1]

[Women] accept the fact that their lives are determined by relationships, that before they are persons, they are somebody's wife, somebody's mother.

—Abigail McCarthy[2]

Let [the man] stand to the woman in the same relation as Christ to His community by being to her the head in this sense, by being genuinely strong and kind in relation to her! If the woman understands the man's precedence and superiority in this sense, in the light of his task and function she will surely be willing not merely to accept but freely to embrace the subordination which befits her.

—Karl Barth[3]

"Dwindling" into a wife takes time. It involves a redefinition of the self and an active reshaping of the personality to conform to the wishes or needs or demands of husbands. . . . This Pygmalion effect [where husbands make wives over to their own ideal] tallies with the finding generally reported that wives make more of the adjustments called for in marriage than do husbands.

—Jessie Bernard[4]

> The women of the nineteenth century were treated in a manner not unlike that which is still the bitter experience of the Negro in many parts of the world. Traits that are mythically attributed to the Negro at the present time were for many generations saddled upon women, the second-class citizens of a patriarchal society.
>
> —Ashley Montagu[5]

> The distinctively masculine characteristics of activity and overt aggressiveness seem to be becoming less useful than the traditionally feminine characteristics of manipulative beguilement or conciliation of other people. Thus, it becomes more difficult to establish a distinctively masculine identity in other than purely sexual terms.
>
> —Hendrik Ruitenbeek[6]

Male and female are not only sexual facts, but also apply to sexual roles. Beyond that, male and female refer to a class within a class. The roles are not always the same in the different economic or racial groups but, in general, women are treated as second class wherever they are and are supposed to exist primarily for male comfort. This is a "wall of hostility" that prevents shalom. It is antishalom and must come down if we are to reach that shalom vision where "there is neither male nor female" (Galatians 3:28).

The sexual division of labor is in many ways comparable to the division of labor based on a caste system, but it is far older and is characteristic of quite primitive societies. We have come to believe that this is the order of creation, as Karl Barth asserts more strongly than most Christian theologians, who simply took the fact of patriarchy, male domination, for granted.[7]

But suppose the method that Paulo Freire worked out applies here. Suppose that the caste system is man-made. There is evidence that the earliest societies were matriarchal and that women were the mothers and founders of civilization. In this case, women are no longer the second sex, but the first sex.[8] If the present structure of male-female roles and relationships has grown up and changed over the years, they can also be transformed in history. Both men and women can ask about the experienced slavery of sex roles in our society and about more adequate forms for both roles.

What sorts of slavery, of oppression, and of repression do men experience as men, in their marriage, in their work, in the expectations society has of them? What kinds of indignities do women experience from the implicit apology of having to admit that one is "just a housewife" or has a second-rate job where one's gifts are always underestimated? What do women resent in men? What do men resent in women? Is the "battle of the sexes" inevitable? Or can the wall of hostility come down?

We find ourselves in a society very much in transition. For some people, rigid sexual stereotypes of men as aggressive and dominating and of women as gentle and self-sacrificing still survive. For others, there is an increasing variety of male and female models or new styles of living. Yet even those who are defining their personal identity outside of the old stereotypes discover the hold on themselves of outmoded social, economic, political expectations and structures. Only gradually do we become aware of them and deal with them. For example, so-called liberated women may still assume that housework is their job and feel guilty when the house doesn't look as they think it should. Men who have come a long way often assume that housework is their wife's job, and that they are doing her a favor by helping, even when both have full-time jobs. Another example is that even those religious denominations which allow the ordination of women have very few places for them to work in ministry. Theory is one thing; the practical reality is another.

In this chapter, we shall (1) name the socialization processes of men and of women, that is, the conditioning or learning of social roles that are all-pervasive in the society's institutions. We will (2) analyze the relationship of sexual role to identity and (3) envision how people begin to liberate themselves from narrow definitions of themselves. We shall then consider briefly the biblical resources to see what insights we may gain from the idea of Jesus as New Person and as a sign of a new relationship between the sexes in the larger community. Finally, we shall (4) reflect on some of the doable actions that may begin to create a new sense of dignity and freedom for both women and men.

NAMING THE PROBLEM

Each of us is constantly forced to meet the expectations of others around us, first of parents, then teachers, then peers, and then the larger society. Males are socialized into one set of possibilities, while females are socialized into a different set. Men are supposed to be strong and in control of themselves emotionally at all times. Men are not supposed to cry. By contrast, women are allowed to be weak, are pliant and are trained to be dependent and to please others. They are emotionally expressive, and they cry. They need someone to lean on, to look up to, and to look after them. Whereas men are supposed to be rational and in control of the public world and of other people (more or less), women are supposed to be intuitive and sympathetic. They are supposed to seek their fulfillment and their identity in the private world of the home. Men work, compete, and find their worth in the competitive worlds of business or politics. Women work at home, take care of children, and find their worth through their husbands. If they work outside the home, their work must always come after their families and is, in fact, a continuation of what they do in the home.

These male and female stereotypes in fact represent two halves of a single human being. At the same time, by representing opposite values, these two half-beings are contradictory. What is labeled female or feminine is by definition second rate and excluded from the public world of men. A man who has "feminine" qualities of intuition, who finds human relationships especially important or who is devoted to the creation of beautiful things is considered to be "effeminate" (a term of insult). By contrast, a woman with a good mind and education is told, "You think like a man" (a compliment). But if she is strong and exercises power, she is often called cruel names, a "castrating bitch" or a "butch." Men and women who do not live up to sex role expectations are suspect by many people.

However, because our society is in transition, people are in transition also. Increasing numbers of men and women are exploring and trying out the strengths of their own temperament and education. The experimentation involved in women learning about automobiles, or girls trying out for the Little League, or boys trying crocheting or creative work with their hands can create a sense of openness and of variety.

However, the mass media provides a pretty accurate reflection of our society and of the images of men and women that still prevail. Newspapers and TV commentators describe and picture men making decisions, doing the important tasks of society, *manning* flights to the moon. Men run government, set price controls or lift them, while women appear on television pushing the shopping carts in the supermarkets. For the most part, men's sports are reported, while women's sports are often overlooked. Most newscasters are men. They report war, murders, robberies, the stock market, and the buying and selling of money.

What is not reported? Community building, ways that people meet their problems in cities and rural areas, new discoveries, art, and poetry. Ordinary people, Black people, women—all are seen as minority people in the home, as domestic workers (advertising the miracle floor wax, though even here it is often a man who speaks authoritatively to the woman). Women are secretaries, nurses, assistants everywhere to men, validated by their service to men.

The stress on patterns of male domination, power, and control come to a high point in our image of the United States and its President. It is assumed that the United States must be first. But first in what? In compassion for the less privileged? In assistance to other countries? In the quality of life within the country? In the beauty of its cities and the creativity of its people? No, America must be first in military might and in wealth. The presidency must be strong as befits a great nation. The President must not give in to pressure, he must not weaken, he must exercise supreme power, in spite of the theory of checks and balances on which the country was founded.

ANALYZING THE PROBLEM

Men: the Myth and Burden of *Machismo*

The emphasis on masculine power and control has been a part of the frontier myth from the beginning of the country. But it is not confined to the United States. Obviously it is still very much a part of European culture. In the Latin cultures that gave it the name *machismo,* the male myth is more closely related to sexual virility and to physical strength than to cold rationality as it is in this country. Today this ideal of masculinity is being increasingly questioned by both men and women. Has there been an overemphasis on masculine values to the exclusion of the feminine values? Have these male values created a world of exploitation and of war? Would feminine qualities help us to be more caring for health, beauty, creativity? Would the killing begin to cease if males were permitted to be less tough and more humane?

THE MALE IMAGE

What does the masculine set of values honor? It honors the possession of strength, the ability to work and provide, the ability to take one's place in the public world as a professional, and the achievement of economic power and political power. These values represent an ascending hierarchy for men.

1. Male Strength. Sheer physical strength is low on the scale of masculine values. This is the kind of strength of the slave, or the truck driver, the lifeguard, or the Black male as whites have seen him and put him down. There is an ambivalence about this kind of power, because it suggests sexual power. In middle aged, upper- and middle-class whites, this physical strength is equated with a kind of raw sexuality that is attributed to the lower class.[9] It is both admired and denigrated.

The athlete is a special case. His skill puts him in a class by himself, and the monetary rewards raise his social position.

2. Male Sexuality as Power. Men are supposed to have a "right" to sex within marriage, while women are expected to want to be dominated by male power. For the "virile" man, every woman is fair game and (he thinks) wants to be conquered. Some men do not seem to believe that rape occurs. Some months ago, for example, in Trenton, New Jersey, a woman was raped on a bridge in sight of several workmen. When the men were questioned about the incident, they said they thought the couple was having intercourse. If it had been rape, they said, the woman would have put up a struggle. According to the woman, she was tripped and pinned to the ground.[10]

If sex is power for men, the reverse is also true. Power itself has sexual overtones. According to Henry Kissinger, power is the "ultimate aphrodisiac." For many men, the power-sex model is sadistic. For a man deprived of power at work or in the public world, wife and family can become the people over whom he can exercise the power he is denied in the world outside. At least at home he is "lord of the castle."

3. Male Power to Work and to Provide. On the masculine scale of values, income and the standard of living (the external sign of income), are valued highly. A man's worth hinges on his ability to bring in more money as he rises up on the ladder of status. By the same token, when he reaches the point of no further advancement, he sometimes begins to experience depression and a loss of manhood. The work becomes a dead end. The internal rewards that might have made the work valuable in itself are often subordinated to the external financial reward.

The definition of a man by his work and ability to provide can create a situation of slavery for men. As the needs of the family increase, he is more tied to his work than ever. He may have to work overtime or to take two jobs if the family is large. He may feel that his family no longer sees him as a person, but merely as one who provides the means for the rest of them to live in leisure. In a perceptive article, Michele Murray comments on Bill Loud in the

Public Broadcasting Service television production, *An American Family*, "For Bill, money-making [as a manufacturer of equipment for strip mining] is a desperate pursuit which is taken for granted or mocked by his children." And he is one of the privileged few who make upward of $20,000.[11]

4. Strength as Power to Dominate Others. One reason why physical strength is not particularly admired today is that it allows only a minimal degree of control over others. A man is more admired the more he has others under him, the more others look up to him. Powerful men like Mayor Daley of Chicago are admired for their control of people. Vicarious identity makes up for people's sense of uncertainty and powerlessness. The bomber pilot's task is another expression of vicarious power. He doesn't even feel his own power, but only responds to his duty and feels that he is doing a "job." The real power is exercised by the man at the head of government who in the worst tradition of machismo exercises superhuman amounts of power. Our presidents promise us that they will never allow America to become a second-rate power. Such power is the power to destroy and to dominate, the epitome of the masculine values honored by the country. Yet we are second rate in many other areas, such as health care, that women tend to value highly.

5. Professional Power. There are some exceptions to the rule of male equals strong, it would appear. Professional men and academic men are not where they are because of their physical strength or domination. Doctors take care of people, which is presumably a feminine attribute. College professors teach literature and art as well as engineering, and may be more gentle than other men. But this is only a surface appearance. There is a whole mentality of machismo in the professions that again functions to glorify male values, the male half of the human set of possibilities. Let us see how machismo works in the professions.

Professional men take pride in their professional status as an in-group, as opposed to the out-group of patients or clients, the laity. In medicine, psychiatry, and ministry, they play the role of the all-knowing father while patients are in effect children who do not know, who are kept mostly in the dark. In psychiatry and the ministry, the professional is more often male, and the client is more often female. It is no accident that many men find it hard to seek the help of a psychiatrist or a minister, because such help would put the male in a child-woman-dependent role.

The professional male gains status both from his increased specialization and from the fees that he charges.[12] One study showed that medical students' motivation was suspect if it was defined in terms of helping people and that the "correct" motivation was to make money. Specialized service has a high price and is available to the few. Preventive medicine and quality health care, which are the citizen's right in most industrialized countries in Europe, are not readily available in this country.[13]

Professionalism has its machismo character. Women find it very difficult to enter most professions. The women's counterpart of medicine is nursing—less professional, less well-paid, and consequently less valued. The counterpart of the psychiatrist is the psychiatric social worker who most often is female. The female counterpart of the minister is the director of Christian education, or in some instances the minister's wife. Again, the female counterpart is nonprofessional. The machismo of the professional male must be described in terms of professional competency rather than in overtly political terms.

Another source of the professional's power is his "detached" and "objective" intellect, which puts his field of specialty somewhere "out there" as an object of study, totally subject to his personal control alone. Thus poverty is not seen as something that people experience as daily defeat, but as an abstraction for the professional politician or poverty worker to control. Often the professional ends up hiring his services out to the highest bidder, and his pose of being objective hides the very real political commitments that he has to his own privileged status in a technological society.[14] Not only does he refuse to question the hidden value structure for himself, but he makes it impossible for anyone else to do so, because that would imply that he is responsible to people in general, and not merely to the elite who can afford to hire him. In a world of technicians and professionals, the ordinary citizen is powerless. Thus, machismo and social exploitation support one another.

6. Manhood, Mastery, and Capital. Making a fortune is a sign of a masculine strength, whether the fortune is made by the president of an oil company, a politician, a doctor, or a physicist. The union boss also is a big man, because his union pays him big money.

7. The Supremacy of Political Power. All the financial powers of the country converge in political power. Wealthy men buy ambassadorial posts for themselves or for their wives; men move from top positions in the CIA to top positions in ITT and back, or from positions in the Food and Drug Administration to the presidency of one of the big drug companies. Power as domination means that there is ultimately only one man whose will really counts, one man who treats all other men in his administration as his own mouthpiece. They say his word but have no voice of their own. Sources of power in the military and in the business world may influence the supreme man, the President, but they must be able to offer something in return.

Competition belongs to power at every level in our society and is characteristic of every sort of male power. The picture of power in traditional terms is the pyramid, where the many at the bottom have little power, little money, and where the few at the top have increasing power and wealth at their disposal. The gap between those at the bottom and those at the top increases year by year. The top of the pyramid is studded with those men who have managed to win the game of "survival of the fittest."

LIBERATION FOR MEN

Liberation is clearly not only for women. Subservient men are in many ways the "women" of society. The more all-male the group is, the more the subservient males take the female position. As one GI on Vietnam duty put it, "We are the officers' women. They've got us." Gloria Emerson, the reporter to whom the comment was made, adds:

> I have never known a woman who was as helpless as a draftee, as humiliated and hassled as he is, or one who had so few choices. Men may be condescending to women, *but they do not send us out to die for them.* The real victims of men are other men.[15]

If there really is only one top man, or a top few men in the United States, how do the rest of the men define themselves as men? They do it vicariously for the most part. Physical strength allows a man to dominate—or to think he dominates—his family. He can prove his superior strength over his wife and children. He identifies himself vicariously with the maleness of the athlete by watching the Sunday football game.

It should be clear from what has been said, however, that the machismo ideal is the result of a sales job on the American male. It is a cover-up that hides the real powerlessness that men have in our society.[16] What is most serious about the myth of machismo is that, for many powerless men, it provides a false identity and a false security—that is, a false shalom. The consequence of this false identity is that they become weaker and less able to act. To question this false identity becomes more and more threatening. One reason why so many men have feared the women's movement is that it has exposed the pain that lies beneath this false identity.

To begin to regain real power over their own lives, men will have to face their own powerlessness and come to understand how machismo has messed up their lives. Men have sold themselves to a set of values that are as destructive of their dignity as they are of the dignity of women. If men were able to talk to men and to speak out of their own feelings of powerlessness with companions and not competitors, they would be able to begin to take power over their own concerns.

This is beginning to happen. The role of the professional as a career-oriented and detached father figure is being mellowed. Many men have seen it as a mask for privilege, and have sought to use their professional skills for the community as a whole. These persons feel themselves to be part of the community. They are politically conscious persons working for change together with other community members. The concern of these new professionals has been to empower community people, to enable them to make use of professional services according to need and not according to income. In the case of the doctor, the new style of professionalism focuses on sharing knowledge with patients and with community paraprofessionals, emphasizing preventive medicine. It is an egalitarian style, both in the use of first names and in salary. It is no longer "Dr. Smith" who speaks to "Jane" or "John" patient, but Harry Smith who is a person, and a doctor. In some community clinics everyone receives an equal salary, because all contribute their expertise and their energy.

Signs of change among men and their perception of themselves are evident in various places. Younger men are beginning to try out forms of action inconsistent with the machismo myth because they refuse to be programmed according to old, ill-fitting definitions. Men are choosing to teach young children, to work part-time, or to stay home and take care of their children for a year or two. Men are going into social work, nursing, and even secretarial work, once traditionally female roles, just as women are moving into what were traditionally male preserves. The point is not so much the fact of changed roles, but the deeper change, that both men and women sit much more lightly within any role. There is a kind of freedom loosening the mental ball and chain that locks us into work. Even the economic necessity can be broken once people experience the possibility of choice about their standard of living.

As a result of these winds of change, especially as men and women work with questions arising out of the movement for women's freedom, more and more men can allow themselves to be warm and sympathetic and supportive of others, and can work cooperatively rather than competitively. Such men, as they become dissatisfied with the emotional deadness of their work, try to integrate their lives, their minds, their feelings, and their sexuality.

Women: Bound Feet and Clipped Wings

Most of what has been written about women until fairly recently has been written by men. The mass media has projected the image of woman as "nun, witch and playmate" or the girl of the ads.[17] An old Geritol TV commercial is one of the more offensive examples of the female image. It portrays the "girl" who is worker, housewife, mother, twin to her teenage daughter, companion and nurse to her father/husband. Of course he'll keep her! He has a bargain, for she makes no claims for herself.

THE FEMALE IMAGE

To explore the way women have been socialized and conditioned, I propose that we examine the prevailing image women have of themselves, the image they try to create in their mirrors as they make themselves up and over. Then we can look at this image and see how we feel about it.

1. Woman/Child. In past years, women have been treated and humored as children. They have assumed an air of wide-eyed innocence and intellectual incompetence. Their dependence claims the care of strong fathers and husbands who feel more masculine because of the care they give these gentle, helpless creatures. This childlikeness went with a woman's inability to support herself in a day when women could not easily find adequate jobs. The financial dependence is still there when a woman has small children, because the economic and social situation is still inadequate for women. Along with the air of dependence, both financial and physical, there is also an emotional dependence. Women are not expected to mature, to be in control of themselves emotionally as men are. Women, like children, cry when they are hurt. Men do not, at least according to the myth.

Women are protected from risks from childhood on—risks that men are expected to take as a matter of course. Women marry for security and a home. They need not compete there or meet a rigid schedule. They may or may not put in an eight-hour day. The time and energy that a woman expends at home will depend largely on the number of small children she has.

The romantic stories of the soap operas that feed women audiences express this fantasy of the child/woman saved and taken care of by the Prince Charming/father image. There is another way of reading this fantasy, however; a woman may feel an intense need to be a child and to be cared for, because in the reality of the home she is woman/mother. She is the person who exists to fill up everyone else's needs, never to think of her own, and in fact to feel guilty if she makes claims about her own needs.

Times have changed for most women, however. The change is illustrated in interviews with some wives of Vietnam prisoners of war. They often stressed the theme of the child/wife of the old days who has become a woman/person, and the problems this would cause their husbands on their return. One woman, Kay, was a dependent, passive child/woman when her husband left for Vietnam. She was "twenty-eight going on seventeen," having in effect stopped growing as a person when she dropped out of high school to get married at age sixteen. During the seven years her husband was away, Kay had the full responsibility for the family and could no longer depend on her husband to make decisions. She felt guilt and fear, because she and the children had grown as people, and she was afraid that her husband would expect them to be pretty much as he left them, when he made all the decisions, when he did not like his wife to read too much or his children to say "Dangit." [18]

2. Woman/Mother. The characteristic of mother is that she is always there for everyone else's needs and never for her own. She feeds the baby when he cries, she is home when children return from school, full of the news of the day, she is there to comfort her husband when he comes in from a hard day's work. But there is no one to hear about her day. What is worse, the woman/mother feels guilty if she is not at everyone else's beck and call. After all, a woman's life is giving according to the role assigned her. So she is cook, dishwasher, waitress, chauffeur, nurse, mistress, cleaning woman, and secretary.

As women grow older, the "empty nest" syndrome lays a heavy hand on them. Many women experience intense depression at this time, because their whole reason for living has gone. This sense of loss is not unlike the sense of loss that men experience at retirement, except that it usually happens earlier for women. The fact that this feeling is also tied up with the physical changes of menopause makes a woman very vulnerable at this time of her life in a man's world. Many women have never asked themselves what they really want in life. When they can say what they need, they can find ways of fulfilling themselves. Then they have some energy to take care of others without being drained by them, or without allowing them to make impossible demands. Having their own emotional needs met as women means that women need not require from children what children cannot give, fulfillment. Children then have more freedom themselves to become different from parents, to become themselves. Women then need not define themselves as mothers only, but can explore themselves as persons.

A partnership marriage, egalitarian in style, is one possible alternative to this wall of sexism. In such a relationship, two mature and equal people can share responsibility both for financial support and for child care. Both can work part-time, or one can work outside, while the other takes responsibility for the children. Or both can work shorter hours, while children have day care, which can help the children to grow. If such a couple is part of a larger communal group, where each person has his or her own friends, then the prevailing condition of psychic scarcity can be dealt with. Each is strong enough to express personal needs. Instead of being trapped by a sense of loneliness, each has a circle of friends beyond the spouse. The two need not be everything for each other, and in this kind of partnership, the relationship is in fact enriched.[19]

3. Woman/Assistant/Wife. If a woman chooses to work in the male world, the role that is waiting for her is the role of assistant. Women usually are nurses assisting doctors who have power and status, secretaries to important male executives, teachers of young children, or administrators at the lower levels of school hierarchy. Men teach adolescents and young adults for the most part, and are the top school administrators.

The woman is also assistant in her husband's work. She takes care of all the day-to-day chores of living—cleaning, cooking, and mothering the children—while her husband is freed for his work. She is also hostess and secretary for him, as well as public relations person. As one talented woman, Abigail McCarthy, put it: "It was what I really wanted to do more than anything else, to be totally part of Gene's life, to make my talents serve his which I thought of as totally unique."[20] Elsewhere she writes in her story of that life of abnegation, "I do not regret that for thirty years, in the words of Simone de Beauvoir, 'I spontaneously preferred another existence to my own.' "[21] The book describes the life of this woman wholly in terms of her husband. She is a loving woman who discovers herself perhaps only when her husband leaves her. Her pattern of unquestioning loyalty, as she looks back on it from the vantage point of the present, has been tried and found wanting.

As assistants, women are not expected to take initiative. Woman/assistants are supportive and noncompetitive. They have been taught to cooperate with men and to follow their initiatives. As wives, they are expected to have no interests of their own, but solely to further the interests of their husbands. Basically, this has to do with the different perception of marriage for her and for him. For her, marriage is a *completion of her personality.* By herself she is basically incomplete, she thinks, and others think. The traditional form of marriage deprives married women of a very real freedom they had before marriage—freedom to operate as an independent person in the economic sphere, in her own name, to pursue her own professional advancement, to work at public affairs as she thinks fit. Married, she has credit cards in her husband's name. In many states she cannot sign for a mortgage by herself, even if she is working and her husband is not. Her job is often not taken seriously by her employer or by her husband for the most part. She is expected to insist that as much as she enjoys her job, her family comes first. By contrast, a married man has the same freedom in the job market as he had before marriage. He is expected by his employer, and he expects himself, to take his job seriously.

4. Woman/Mannequin. As men see women, they describe this aspect of woman as "Playmate" or as "Temptress" depending on their point of view. From a woman's point of view, however, she is a "mannequin" because her job is continually to make herself over in order to be attractive to men and envied by other women. Women work hard at "making themselves up." There is a real self-hatred implied in the constant effort to make one's face over by make-up, one's body over by endless dieting and exercising. Woman/mannequin is a work of art.

The purpose of this artistic creation is twofold: it is a way of gaining attention from men, but even more it is a way of gaining identity. Many women see themselves as persons through their appearance, not through their interests or activities or achievements. Even—or perhaps particularly—talented and intelligent women strain to be beautiful according to the false standard of a society that imposes the same style on all women.

There is a trend, however, for women to accept themselves as they are in their infinite variety. Fashion pages are showing styles designed for women as they are actually shaped, not as they ought to be shaped. Although they don't yet show models in those shapes, there is a slogan claiming, "Big Is Beautiful." [22]

These four roles of child, mother, assistant, and mannequin are not entirely unsatisfactory to women. A good number of women are protesting the equal rights amendment because they fear the loss of their right to support from their husbands. These women may fear the competitive work world or do not want to be tied down to work on a nine-to-five basis as men are. To the extent that women have a choice that their husbands do not have—to work outside the home or not, especially as children grow older—they are indeed freer than their husbands. They may or may not be developed as persons. In any case, liberation is for men as well as for women.

THE EFFECTS OF DEPENDENCE

The real cost of the kind of slavery that results from roles which lock in people is its dependence. Dependence cripples people and prevents personal and social growth. Both men and women are crippled to the extent that these superimposed roles lock them in—to the extent that understanding, freedom and love are cut off by mind-numbing routine and heart-killing overwork. Men are crippled because their jobs deaden their sensitivities and kill their interest and enthusiasm when work becomes a treadmill.

Women tend to be crippled by a long-standing distrust of their own power outside the home. They are crippled to the extent that they are easily discouraged and are afraid of taking risks. They are crippled to the extent that they cannot be comfortable with who they are. As they grow older, they are crippled by the knowledge that the battle to stay young is being lost every day. It is small comfort to be told after your fortieth birthday, "You don't look that old!" In addition to discrimination against women (sexism), women are particularly vulnerable to discrimination against age (ageism).[23]

The inner reality of dependence is fear and depression. When women begin to deal with their own feelings about their social conditioning, they discover depression, anger, and fear. Depression is usually the mask of anger turned against oneself.

Fear takes many forms for women. Sometimes it is fear of unknown responsibility. It is often fear of speaking out in public, because women have learned their place too well. In public they are expected to be silent. (See 1 Corinthians 14:34.) It is easier to allow men to speak, because men consistently have more opportunity and encouragement to speak than women do. When women become angry enough, however, then they speak up and speak out. It is curious that people who are sympathetic to the Black struggle and to the new articulateness of Black people cannot understand women in a comparable situation. Women who are angry are called "strident."

Anger, however, may be the only motivation strong enough to overcome fear. Women tend to be more fearful of breaking the law than men. They are more docile and find it harder to leave home than their brothers do because their conditioning is to a dependent existence.

Even when a law is understood to be unjust, it takes a long period of "de-conditioning" for women to overcome their fear. Because of women's experience of oppression and perhaps because of their own sensitivities (whether native or learned), women find it easier to care for the underprivileged, the deprived in society. Here too, however, they usually do not become sufficiently involved to challenge the status quo.[24]

If women are in leadership positions, are strong and intelligent in a position where they not only compete with men but also can exercise power, they still are not free from fear. The fear may become greater because now they have to deal with the contradiction between their masculine success and their feminine identity.

It is little wonder then that at best women are ambivalent about success, and at worst actively fear it. Psychologist (and recent president of Radcliffe College) Matina Horner tested Radcliffe women and discovered that they score high on anxiety in the face of success. Radcliffe women are in fact selected on the basis of intelligence and are among the most intelligent women in the whole country. But with regard to the success that they can well expect, they are confused because they receive contradictory signals. On the one hand, they can and do achieve, while on the other, they themselves see unusual excellence in a woman as loss of femininity. They fear both social rejection and loss of personal well-being.

In the Horner study both men and women were asked to complete one-sentence story lines. For the men the story was given as follows: "After first term finals, John finds himself at the top of his medical school class . . ." Men completed the story by describing success in their careers, ability to support a wife and family. For women, the name "Anne" was substituted for "John," and the sequels are very different. One woman completed the story thus:

> Anne starts proclaiming her surprise and joy. Her fellow classmates are so disgusted with her behavior that they jump on her in a body and beat her. She is maimed for life.

Another woman student told the story a different way:

> Anne will deliberately lower her academic standing the next term, while she does all she subtly can to help Carl. . . . His grades come up and Anne soon drops out of medical school. They marry and he goes on in school while she raises their family.[25]

Women even more than men have been conditioned to weakness, to fear, and to dependence by a system of rewards and punishments that is still in operation.[26] Women (and men) can simply continue to accept that conditioning, or they can examine it critically to decide where they need to decondition themselves, to work to become whole persons, free of the fear that has crippled them for so long a time. Deconditioning will mean facing the fear, itself a frightening thing. It will mean living with fear and with frustration and discovering ways of acting around it. Deconditioning will also have to come to grips with the fact that the depression so many women and men live with is the consequence of anger turned against oneself, instead of against the situation that inspired the anger. Until people learn to be angry, to overcome their own self-hatred, they will not be able to move ahead.

ENVISIONING ALTERNATIVES

Dependence is a pervasive theme in our lives and is to be distinguished from interdependence, which is a healthy form of relationship, where we both give and receive, where others make claims on us, and yet where we maintain our own integrity as persons. Dependence has been an essential theme in women's analysis of their own situation, as we have seen. It is also a basic theme in the analysis of social structures and class structures. Recently, in Latin American theology, dependence has also become a theological theme. Gustavo Gutierrez defines the condition of poverty and powerlessness in so much of Latin America as a situation of sin, because it is a situation of dependence.[27] As we shall see later, sin is located in the social structures that destroy people.

Liberation itself becomes an active participation in the redemptive process. The struggle for liberation here is something more than conversation, which would affect only one's own self. Liberation is a struggle that must involve whole communities of people if it is to be real. Women's liberation is in some ways not unlike the Latin American struggle for liberation. There are many analogies that can be drawn.

No one can go through this kind of deconditioning alone. Breaking out of these roles even in psychological therapy leaves one too isolated, especially if therapy aims to change only the person and not the walls of hostility between men and women. It is no accident that the women's movement has grown out of support groups originally dealing with personal issues. As women talked to one another, they discovered that these personal issues were in fact social and political in their importance. The problem was not the women but the social conditions. By and large, most people blame themselves for what goes wrong, and not the conditions. Deconditioning will require a supportive group where people share some common experiences that lead to shared reflection and, above all, to action.

A New Marriage

Men and women each pay a high price for marriage. For both it may lead to a kind of dependence that can be crippling in different ways. For women, however, the price generally has been considerably higher than the price that men have paid. As men and women ask themselves what they really want of marriage, they can begin to share their dreams with each other, and develop new forms of marriage relationships—as many as there are people. Ideally, the form of marriage that allows for both freedom and growth is a marriage where the two are friends as well as lovers. In such a marriage, both have equal claims and equal rights.

Each partner has a job that the other partner considers as important as his or her own. Or either has a chance not to be employed, while the other takes over the responsibility of providing. Each takes an interest in the other's work. If the work requires moving for either of the two, this is negotiable. Housework is shared, unless one really enjoys it. When children come, they are part of the family, but the family does not revolve around them alone.

Can a new style of marriage work? It can indeed, though couples are very conscious of a whole new learning process as they work on problems together.

In one case, Jim is a graduate student, while Linda is a consultant to an educational corporation. As she has become aware of her own gifts and of discrimination against her as a woman, she has become more enterprising and more determined. Urged on by Jim, she has taken on more responsibility. After he finishes his graduate studies, they are planning to stay on where they are, so that she can explore new developments in her job. This is partly because jobs in his area of specialization are scarce, but partly because he feels it is her turn to do what she wants to do. In two or three years, he will look for a job, and she will be ready to move into something different herself—either to have children or to go on for further study. For them, the future is open.

Jesus, the New Person

The Christian community has usually understood Jesus from the viewpoint of his masculinity. The churches have been historically dominated by men in power, using Jesus to justify this actual exercise of power. But Jesus himself does not fulfill the machismo ideal at all. He rejects domination as the mode of relationship and of action for his followers. They are not to be lords, masters, teachers, nor even fathers with authority. All these things belong to God. They are rather to serve and to be like the youngest (Luke 22:25ff). Jesus rejects for his followers the mode of power that is domination. Such power conflicts with his own vocation to speak the truth that liberates people. When he speaks about freedom, and the early Christian community applies it, it is not about some vague, disembodied spiritual freedom, but about the freedom of real people, so that their lives no longer have to be determined by the principalities and powers—that is, the actual powers of the Roman occupation and of the local collaborators. (See Matthew 22:21; Ephesians 6:12; Colossians 2:15.)

The problem is that Jesus and the apostles often become models for the very type of oppressive rule and control that Jesus himself so often protested and against which he struggled. Oppressive power has been a temptation of the Christian church in the hierarchical structures that have rewarded the affluent and deprived the weak, that have deprived minority groups of a voice, and that have monopolized power for males.

Jesus himself exercised power very differently. He did not seek to impose his will on others, to brainwash or control them. For him, power was new life, new energy, new hope in a vision, which he shared initially with a tiny community. He came to build a community that could manifest the shalom of God by giving power to people to help them grow and develop, to grow up to the full measure of their humanity. (See Ephesians 4:11–16.) Part of the maturity of the community could come only when he was no longer physically present, so that others could share leadership with him.

Women have had a special problem with the theology of Jesus and of the Christian community, especially as they have begun to define their own needs and their own oppression in contemporary society. As we reread the New Testament, we become aware of the patriarchal society of the time, and the male-dominated mind set of the New Testament writers themselves. But not only that. We become aware also in the early Christian community of the problem that women were creating because they took literally the gospel of liberation. Women were very active in the community. The peak moments of women's ministry were Mary's function as an archetypal Christian person, the ministry of Mary of Bethany, the apostolic ministry and witness of the women at the resurrection, and last but not least, the women who prophesied at Corinth. When Paul recommended to the Corinthian women that they not speak in the church and that they wear veils, I suggest that Paul was experiencing the power of the new wine of the Christian spirit and it frightened him! Somehow he had to get Christian women back into the safe patterns of womanly submission. But this is Paul speaking, not Jesus. And it is not Paul at his best.

Is today not a time when the breakdown of the old calls for a new style, a new understanding, a new look at the vision of shalom, where there is no dominance of male or female?

DOABLE ACTIONS

Establish a Women's Support Group

Support groups provide a context for examining the conditioning we have all been subjected to and for beginning to decondition ourselves, both in our personal stance and in our interpersonal and public actions. As women we can learn to express our strong feelings, our anger, and not just smile or be excessively tactful. We can insist.

But such a group goes beyond the personal and, in fact, shows up the political dimensions of personal struggle. Such a group can help deal with concerns like the following:

—dissatisfaction with present roles.

—feelings of anger, guilt, depression, shame.
—learning to put feelings into words and to speak up.
—pushing beyond the personal dimensions of problems. (This is especially important, because whenever anything is made into *your* or *my* personal problem, it appears that there is something wrong with you or me as an individual.)
—an intelligent understanding of the workings of the social *systems* in all their ramifications in our lives. (Only when we begin to investigate do we realize how much we have been kept in ignorance and are, therefore, powerless.)
—effective action, where we begin to learn the power we can have. (Experiment with different forms of action in order to understand the social system better, and in order to make it work for people.)

Join Women's Groups Organized for Effective Action

—Women's Lobby, Inc., 1345 G Street, S.E., Washington, D.C. 20002 (202-547-0082). This lobby works to implement equal rights for women, child care, and pension and social security benefits. The goal is to check all legislation for "feminist impact," for its effects on the lives of women, who are too often hidden in terms of the law.
—National Organization for Women, 1957 E. 73rd Street, Chicago, Illinois 60649. Goals here are similar to the Women's Lobby, in terms of ratification of the equal rights amendment and equal employment, but go beyond them to restructure social organizations and structures. Thus NOW is also working on reorientation of the educational system to eradicate sexist literature and history that makes women largely unimportant and second class. It is also involved in developmental child care and paid maternity leave for working women. NOW also encourages women to participate fully in political activities.
—Women's International League for Peace and Freedom, 1213 Race Street, Philadelphia, Pennsylvania 19107. This is a much older organization of women concerned with issues of peace and freedom dating back to the struggle of women at the beginning of the twentieth century. It is more explicitly concerned with issues of peace and less with women's rights, but obviously the two sets of issues are closely connected.
—Women's Caucuses at the State Level. These are important both for learning about political process as well as for participating in and getting a hearing for women's concerns.

Encourage Women's Medical Self-Help

Although women make 25 percent more visits to doctors than men do, 93 percent of all doctors are male. Many women are beginning to reject the parent-child model that the doctor-patient relationship implies, particularly for women. Self-help clinics focus initially on gynecological treatment where women feel most strongly the indignity of having their bodies controlled by male doctors.[28]

Women are providing other forms of medical assistance. Nurses are going into private practice, where they bring a real concern for the client as person.[29] In the future, such nurse practitioners (male as well as female) may revolutionize the practice of medicine by focusing on preventive medicine—teaching clients to take care of their own bodies, to understand the healing process, and to see the importance of good nutrition for good health. In addition, these nurse practitioners visit the home in case of need, a practice most doctors long since have given up.

Renegotiate the Marriage Contract

As women discover their own whole personhood, their gifts and talents in the public world of work and politics, they are no longer the same women their husbands married. As men discover their slavery to work structures growing out of the male head-of-the-family and provider role, they too can explore alternative styles together with women. Marriage becomes then a partnership of equals, open to change and growth.[30]

When measured against the vision of shalom, the walls of hostility dividing the male-female community are hard to tear down. However, the recent consciousness of the exploitation of women and its by-product of male awareness of his absurd machismo role is very encouraging.

When we look closely at the image of Jesus, we do not find a tough cowboy character who wins by defeating others, but a man whose power makes us all powerful.

CHAPTER 4
THE FAMILY AND WHOLE COMMUNITY

Families are in trouble in America because they have been sold a set of values that is both contradictory and fraudulent. They have been whipped into zealous profit-making and accumulation (thus rending man from woman and parent from child) and taught at the same time that the family should be a sunny island of warmth and bliss in a cold sea of cruelty and competition. The church has exacerbated the contradiction by withdrawing its concern for humanizing the public realm and concurrently laying onto the diminishing family a set of expectations so high that the Holy Family itself would now be viewed with suspicion by psychological counselors.

—Harvey Cox[1]

The conviction of a family that it is the whole social arena in microcosm limits the experience of family members in both an obvious and subtle way. It is clear that no congeries of four or five people represent the full spectrum of attitudes and human traits to be found in the wider society. Family reality, therefore becomes highly exclusive.

—Richard Sennett[2]

The family [is] a unit of repression, a unit of the machinery that is declaring itself omnipotent, a unit of the consumer society, a unit of the warmaking society.

—Daniel Berrigan[3]

War is not good for children and other living things.

—Peace Motto

Liberated women? Yes? . . . Women liberated *for* families and husbands and community, rather than from some bondage. Liberated to experience a fuller sexuality, an authentic femininity, rather than to assume some supposedly "male" roles and functions.

—Lucy Powell[4]

There are many views of the function of the family today. How do you feel about the role of the family? If you were to brainstorm about questions of family structure, what sorts of questions would you come up with? Take a little time with a group of people to get out all your assumptions and questions; put them on newsprint. What are the values implicit in each set of assumptions?

Here are a few for starters:

—Families are breaking down.

—Families are stronger than ever.

—Children don't care about the things their parents struggled for.

—Children are an extension of the parents.

—The family is a miniature community. Learning to live together in the family makes one able to live in the larger society.

—Families are isolated today from the larger community.

—Families are too much turned in on themselves.

—Women's job is to create a harmonious family atmosphere.

—Women's liberation will destroy the family.

—The test of family life is concern for children all over the world.

—The family exists for the sake of the children.

Then turn those statements around into questions: "Are families breaking down?" What does this mean? Individual families? Family life generally? What is the evidence that allows one to make such a generalization? To what extent are particular problems related to the structure of the family in relation to the larger society rather than to the family in and of itself?

From questions like these, we can go on to the action question: To what extent are marriage and family structures oppressive? How can marriage and family living break through oppressive structures to become more liberating for the members of the family as well as contribute to a liberation of people in the larger society? In short, what are the social implications of the family, its outreach to the larger society?

The steps for relating the family to shalom community are: (1) naming the problem of isolation and powerlessness of the contemporary family, (2) analyzing the family as prison/haven and as a public community, and (3) envisioning a family of shalom. The final step is (4) considering actions for expanding possibilities of community.

NAMING THE ISOLATION AND POWERLESSNESS

The family in some form has existed throughout history in every society. It is the basic structure of society because it meets needs for sex, for affection, for the continuation of the race, and also for communal living. The family has taken many forms. In Africa and parts of America, there are polygamous family units, where each mother and her children have their own house. The whole compound is made up of several such units, presided over by the husband and father. He has his own house, with access to each of the other houses. In such societies, there is provision for every woman, and none is left out.[5]

The more common form of the traditional family, even in American society until a generation or two ago, has been the extended family. Here the smaller family of parents and children formed part of the larger family of grandparents, aunts, uncles, cousins, and others of more extended relationships. Unmarried relatives were at home with their married brothers, sisters, nieces, and nephews, and often helped out with their care. Part of the extended family often lived nearby and provided adult companionship for the women in their work. Children grew up in a comfortable atmosphere. They were able to form close relationships with adults other than their parents.

In the early days of American life on the frontier, the family was a production unit. Children were welcomed as additional hands on the farm, and older girls helped their mothers with younger children.

Today, however, the family is no longer a productive unit but a unit of consumption. The father's work is usually away from the family, and the children are the primary responsibility of their mother. The children do not add to the productive capacity of the family, nor to the family income. In fact, the reverse is true in our society. Children have become an expensive item, from medical costs at pregnancy and birth, through the years of schooling, until early youth, when college for each child becomes a major investment. Children are the beneficiaries of a process to which they do not contribute. Their power to earn coincides with their leaving the family home.

What is new about the contemporary family is that the old network of relationships of the extended family has broken down at the same time as we are making greater demands upon the family than ever before. Children require more care and more education, more advantages than ever before. As the family has become smaller, relationships have intensified, because they have become compressed into a smaller space.

For many people, the basic importance of the family is that it is a miniature version of the larger society, a microcosm. The family mirrors the outside world. People learn to get along and are socialized in the family, it is thought, so that they can deal with the world outside. The hidden assumption here is that the world outside has the same kind of uniformity, the same patterns of relationships as the family does. That is, the world outside is basically personal rather than economic or political.

However, to think of the family as a microcosm of the larger world is to falsify both family and world. The family is homogeneous in our society and intensely personal. The larger society is heterogeneous and is structured by other sorts of relationships, business and political. The psychology of large groups is very different from the psychology of the intimate family group.

Richard Sennett claims that the high expectations placed on the family in contemporary society constitute a quest for perfect community, understood as the conquest of conflict and "disorder." It is an attempt to control relationships, to be in a situation where one is always in full control, where one is never surprised, and where the new has no chance to enter. He says:

> In the last few decades, the family has appropriated the social functions and contacts that men once sought in the broader arena of the city. This appropriation by the family of social "spaces" once felt inappropriate has encouraged something perverse in the urban communal relations that men have left and in the family itself. This perversity is a seeking after solidarity and a fear of experiences that might create complexity or disorder.[6]

The search for identity and social unity has led to an unusual fear of uncertainty and of conflict. The small nuclear family is paradoxically stronger than ever. It may even be too strong in its isolation because emotional energies have been invested there to the neglect of the public world.

This isolation in the cities is a relatively new phenomenon, which has developed as city life has become increasingly conflict ridden and complex. In the early years of the century, immigrants moved into the cities, where their lives always overlapped with others, because of living conditions and because of work. Today for the first time, people can afford to live in areas (suburbs or wealthy neighborhoods) composed of "people like us." Isolation has programmed out diversity and variety in favor of a community of similarity, at least for the affluent.

ANALYZING THE FAMILY AS PRISON OR HAVEN

In effect, the family has withdrawn from a world felt to be alien and hostile. The more the home has become a shelter and a haven of personalistic values, the more the family has discovered itself to be isolated and powerless in the outside world.

Isolation and powerlessness do not strike all members of the family equally. Women and children are more isolated than men, because they are more confined to the private world of the home and have few emotional or other resources outside the family circle. Isolation of women from the public life is both a loss to the community and a deep personal loss. Cornell sociologist Andrew Harter puts the matter very strongly: "The trouble in modern family life comes from the fact that the institution we call marriage can't hold two full human beings—it was only designed for one and a half." [7] Women develop in the private sphere in their relationships with only a few people, most of whom are children. Women who are housebound themselves are often frustrated by the feeling of being stunted. The limitations and crippling effects of narrow contacts are, of course, not confined to women. Anyone whose contacts are limited will experience the same stunting of growth.

The loss of women's human gifts is also a loss to the community, which emphasizes so-called male attributes, and downgrades feminine traits. Caring and concern are part of service vocations and are considered to be unrealistic; whereas power, control, and profit are the realistic (and male) forms of public life. The widespread corruption of public officials is but one example of the divorce of the public from the private. Politicians are usually fine family men who compete in a public world where decency is often left at home.

In today's middle-class nuclear family, the care of the children becomes the total responsibility of the parents with little help from the extended family. The more the parents try to be everything and to provide everything for their children, the more they are burdened by a sense of responsibility they can never meet. The reverse side of the picture is that children have the equally heavy responsibility of meeting their parents' expectations, a responsibility that they in turn can never meet. Children become overdependent upon their mothers, and mothers are tied down to their children. This mutual overdependence retards the growth and holds back the energies of both mother and children. Children may in fact do better with less concern and may thrive on new and diverse experiences. It is particularly important for them to have adult figures besides parents to whom they can relate—adult figures who are not authority figures.[8]

The immense concern of modern mothers for the rearing, shaping, and molding of the children focuses the children's attention on themselves as separate entities, rather than as responsible and active members of the community, as participants in an interesting world. Children cease to be reality-centered, and become self-centered. The sheer outgoing energy of children, says Germaine Greer, seems

> diabolical to us, because our whole culture is bent on harnessing it for ulterior ends; the child must be civilized; what that really means is that he must be obliterated . . . the child's attention must be weaned away from exterior reality on to an introverted relationship of mutual exploitation.[9]

The problem here is that both parents and society have increasing expectations of the family. Both parents and children need the support of a larger community of concern, a community that can provide alternatives both for parents and for children.

If a child is locked into a bad home situation and cannot leave because she/he is too young or because there is no place for the child to go, severe personality disorders may develop. British psychiatrist, R. D. Laing studied a number of young women with long histories of schizophrenia. Far from being irrational responses, their symptoms were intelligent responses that made sense in terms of their situations. In describing these young women in the 1950s and 1960s in Britain, he makes it quite clear how they were locked into their families by being excluded from work possibilities outside the home.[10]

The family and the outside world thus often represent contradictory values. In the family the children are taught what are considered to be feminine values, to care for others, to cooperate, to take responsibility for the common work around the house, not to fight. Mothers aim to motivate their children from within to succeed at school. Within the loving atmosphere of the home, children learn to relate to other people, to share justly (more or less of course), and they also learn a sense of religion. Sex education (or lack of it) is the prerogative of the home.

Some parents have attempted to communicate their own social concerns to their children—concerns of poverty, injustice, racism, and war. Psychologist Kenneth Keniston suggests that it is the social and moral concern of the parents that inspired many youth in the 1960s to the kind of political action that so disturbed their parents.[11] Whereas the parents were content to have the right attitudes and to communicate those attitudes to their children, the children translated these attitudes into action. What was a social concern for their parents became for the children a contradiction between what was *said* at home and *done* in public.

Some of these young people are also becoming dissatisfied with the smallness and isolation of the nuclear family. Their disillusionment, says Germaine Greer, has

> revealed the function of the patriarchal family unit in capitalist society. It immobilizes the worker, keeps him vulnerable, so that he can be tantalized with the vision of security. It gives him a controllable pattern of consumption to which he is thoroughly committed.[12]

The isolation of the nuclear family shortchanges the father as well as the mother and children. Men instinctively know this and fear the marriage bond, whereas women in the past have feared being without it. Today some young women are reluctant to enter into this form of family life, because they too see it as a kind of bondage and imprisonment. However, there are alternative life-styles that may free women, men, and children alike. These will be considered later.

ENVISIONING A FAMILY OF SHALOM

In many ways we have not read Jesus' view of the family correctly. Jesus was not a family man, nor were the apostles, in the sense we understand the term. We emphasize the Holy Family as ideal, forgetting that it is but one moment in a continuing story. From the infancy stories to the death and resurrection stories, Jesus is portrayed as one who belongs to his people. Matthew's genealogy makes clear that Jesus is a public personage (Matthew 1). He is described as one who is born away from home. The wise men come to worship him, as a sign of the fact that he belongs to the whole world. The mysterious story in Luke 2:41–52 of the adolescent Jesus in the temple, beginning to take up the adult role, illustrates his public mission.

The teachings of Jesus are also illuminating. When the woman in the crowd raised her voice to praise Jesus and his mother, "Blessed is the womb that bore you, and the breasts that you sucked," Jesus responded, "Blessed rather are those who hear the word of God and keep it" (Luke 11:27–28). In another saying, when Jesus hears that his mother and his brothers wish to see him, he says to the crowd, "My mother and my brothers are those who hear the word of God and do it" (Luke 8:19–21). The Lord's prayer itself makes clear that we are one human family, where no one is master or father but God. (See Luke 22:24–26.) As Jesus goes through the countryside teaching and preaching, one gets the impression that his close family is the small group of men and women who understand him and share his work, and his community and parish are where he finds them, not the family as we now define it.

Roman Catholics have found room for this vision in some measure. They have venerated the sisterhoods and the brotherhoods as a way of living this gospel sense of family. By foregoing their own private families, sisters and brothers find a larger family in the world. For St. Francis, the world of Brother Sun and Sister Moon and the world of the birds and animals were also part of his family. But the Catholic orders have also become privatized and separated from the Catholic lay Christians. As in critical times in the past, new family community experiments have arisen to live out the promise of the early Christian community. Today may be such a critical time. In the same way that the early Christians shared "all things in common" and broke bread together in their homes, witnessing to the power of the Spirit (Acts 2:44–47), the miracle can happen today.[13]

How do we go beyond our families, break out of the cocoon, to become people who care for the public well-being as well as for our private families? How do we become people who create shalom in city neighborhoods, at jobs, among young people, among lonely people wherever they are, among old people, among people who have lost hope? How can we find shalom with other nations? How can we find shalom ourselves?

In the past, churches also have become privatized. They have feared involvement with social issues because of the pervasive problem of the alliance of church and state. Social action was for the most part outside of Christian life and not allowed to displace theology and worship. Churches have traditionally emphasized family life and national life, especially in wartime. Churches have often been isolated groups themselves, composed of people of the same class and economic status. Until the challenge was raised both from within and without, particularly during the civil rights movement, they were able to avoid some of the questions of social justice.

What is not so often seen and understood is that the church's support of the family and emphasis on family life may be a way of distracting attention from pressing social, political, and economic questions. An extreme example is in Brazil, where the oppressive military dictatorship affirmed the traditional church emphasis on family life together with loyalty to the nation. What was less obvious was that the government of Brazil made a concerted effort to break down and destroy intermediate groups that expressed the political interests of the masses of people unrepresented in the government. Thus labor unions in the towns and cities and peasant unions in the countryside were disbanded, as were all political clubs. The student movements in the universities, including the Protestant and Catholic student movements, were annihilated by the arrest and the torture of their leaders. The churches have not responded in any concerted way, so that dissenting church members have been easily isolated and made powerless. Dom Helder Camara, the nonconformist Bishop of Recife, for example, is not allowed to speak on the radio or to write for the newspapers in Brazil, while his associates have been harassed and even murdered, though the government dares not prevent him from speaking all over the world. Everywhere in Brazil people have retreated into their families, as much through the fear of incriminating their friends as through fear for themselves. Some have even become divorced in the effort to secure the safety of their spouses.[14] The church was used to domesticate and privatize all moral concerns by keeping them out of public life and within the family.

In our society, family, church, and gospel have all been relegated to the sphere of the private, perhaps not as drastically as in Brazil, but with some of the same consequences. In North America, it is we ourselves who have privatized the church and the gospel. For many people still, sexual ethics has more to do with the gospel than do social ethics, despite the fact that Jesus himself said very little about sexual issues and much more about poverty, sickness, and social evil. Pornography is more obscene for many people than are napalm burns and dumdum bullets designed to burn and explode human flesh. For these people, ministry belongs only to ordained ministers, who are to take care of people involved in the daily routines of work and family.

Once again, however, the gospel needs to be "publicized," to be spoken and heard outside the sphere of the private. How can we publicize that word and make the word of God active and effective in the public world in a way that affects all of us? We can begin by rejecting the contradiction of the warm, private home versus the cold, oppressive, public world. We can begin by calling into question the rules of public games. We can begin to demand honest, human concern from our officials and to support people with that kind of concern. To assume politics is dirty and corrupt is to indulge ourselves in a self-fulfilling prophecy. To the extent that families and churches have abdicated political responsibility, as was done when Israel turned over all public power to a king, they have contributed to the growth of irresponsible power—that is, power without accountability. To democratize power will mean insisting on accountability by public figures and a new covenant of responsibility by persons and families to the public vision of shalom.

As a child did you ever identify yourself by name at your home address, then go on to expand the circles to include your town, your state, your country, your continent, your planet, your solar system, your galaxy, your constellation? Such an exercise gives a sense of the wholeness of shalom, of which we are a very real part. Looking at the stars and reflecting on the immensity of the universe and the smallness of the human can give one the same feeling. We belong to the whole world and it in turn is part of us. The family, too, is not a whole or a separate reality in itself, but is always a part related to the larger whole. Our thinking about both family and community is complete only when we look at the family's relation to the larger whole, as well as its relation to the individuals within the group.

Family, as I have used it here, refers primarily to the historical structure of the generations—of parents and of children—into which is built both impermanence and permanence. Children grow up, but they always remain the offspring of their parents. To some extent, the hierarchical structures of domination/dependency always remain. In intentional communities, however, people may relate to one another in egalitarian patterns. Community then is built up on the communication and sharing of the members with one another. Community, like family, has both an outward and an inward dimension. Clovis Shepherd estimates that the average time for intragroup concern is about one-third of the total time a group is gathered.[15]

Community and family take time. We need time to learn to talk to one another, to hear one another, and time to act out our new knowledge. They also take energy. Strains like poverty, sickness, and overwork can leave people with little energy and few inner or outer resources to learn the skills of communication in the family. A minimal income and a certain amount of leisure become necessities for the development of human potentialities in family/community life.

Draw an imaginary lifeline, with your birth at one end, the important events that have already happened, and the time you think you have left to live. Our future need not be the same as the past. We can drift unthinkingly and lose time, or we can envision a better future and choose deliberately to create it.

Love openly expressed is a simple way to aim that future toward shalom. Children as well as adults have a great need to be loved, held, and reassured. The pity of it is that our society tolerates this kind of affection only for very small children, and for girls longer than for boys. From childhood on, however, children may live deprived of expressed and tangible warmth until marriage. Perhaps affection more freely expressed can provide the self-affirmation that children, youth, and adults need and can make people more willing to take risks.[16]

When the family breaks down for adults because of the departure of the children, the death of one of the partners, divorce, or simply because one never married, life may be very lonely. American life makes little room for single people, who can be very uncomfortable socially in predominantly couple situations. Singles groups provide some alternative, and communal living provides an even more viable alternative. Others can find the warmth and affection they need in their work, for example, in teaching or in ministry.[17] Loneliness is particularly likely to be the condition of life for older people, especially for women, who outnumber men in the higher age brackets. There are 126 women over the age of 65 to every 100 men. The Beatles' song "Eleanor Rigby" expresses this loneliness.

Loneliness, one of the pervasive experiences of our society, is a sign of the breakdown of family and community relationships. Alternative church ministries can focus on facilitating new communities where lonely people may reconnect with other people of all ages. Such communities can also provide a broader context for families in their isolation. Lonely people can gain a new sense of their own worth as they learn how to minister to others.

Can we release the hidden power of Christian love to create a new world? Can we respond to the needs of others beyond our own families, and to deal "with one another in a way which will make it possible for children to exist throughout the world, for children to thrive, for children to have those decent basic necessities that make for a future?"[18] How, in short, do the emotional resources of the family become available to create a new city, a new world? and how in turn does this concern enrich the family?

SOME PRACTICAL ACTIONS

Learning Groups

1. Bible study groups that seek to explore the meaning of the Bible in contemporary life can become a source of community. If reflection leads to concrete action, the sense of community becomes stronger.

2. Parent effectiveness training groups are sometimes formed in the context of a church or a school. Such groups provide ways for parents to learn effective alternatives to authoritarian ways of dealing with children. These skills can help parents to establish more comfortable parent-child relationships. These groups also function as support groups for parents.[19]

Forms of Communal Living

1. For older people, the Gray Panthers, founded in Philadelphia, have provided both companionship and a base for political action. One of the founders, Maggie Kuhn, who is in her sixties, is deeply concerned about the passive and marginal roles that older people are forced into, as well as the poverty endemic to retirement for many older people. The Gray Panthers won the battle for free checking accounts for senior citizens at The First Pennsylvania Bank, and they will be working closely with Ralph Nader's group to monitor nursing homes.

Another project of concern to Maggie Kuhn is a plan for communal living near the University of Pennsylvania where older and retired people would live together with students. People would have their own apartments, but there would also be a variety of common rooms and facilities where they could mingle freely and get to know each other. For the students, it would provide an opportunity for living in close contact with a nonstudent community and a mixed age grouping. For the older people, it would be a welcome alternative to the age-segregation of old folks homes. It would provide opportunities for the older people to take advantage of the educational resources of the university, as well as of the free university. They would also be able to participate with the students in one or another community action project. The newsletter, *Gray Panthers Network*, may be obtained by writing to: The Gray Panthers, 3700 Chestnut Street, Philadelphia, Pennsylvania 19104.

2. Brotherhood of the Spirit is a community of some 300 people living in four neighboring locations in Vermont. Most of the community's members are in their twenties and thirties, but there are some older members also. This community is a viable alternative to the usual family arrangement. One woman is a widow with grown-up children, while another is a divorcee with children still in school. The group provides these women with a real sense of community they might not have otherwise. Financial resources are shared and are supplemented by a traveling rock band, Spirit in Flesh. Jobs are not given out on the basis of sex roles, but are a matter of choice. There is freedom to move from the leather crafts shop to the vegetable garden or to child care. Some members have outside jobs. Both men and women take responsibility for the children, though small children are looked after mostly by their mothers. The children seem very happy.[20]

3. The Philadelphia Life Center describes itself as "a community of learners experimenting with nonviolent alternatives . . . a community of action joining with others in the Movement for a New Society to aid the growth of creative mass struggle for fundamental social change . . . a community of people learning to care for and share with each other." Their style has grown out of the Quaker heritage, both in the emphasis on nonviolence and the search for truth through the sense of the meeting. Further information may be obtained from: Training Collective, 1006 S. 46th Street, Philadelphia, Pennsylvania 19143.

4. *Los Muchachos* is a Spanish version of Father Flanagan's Boys Town and was inspired by it, though it has a very different flavor. It began when a Spanish priest took homeless boys off the streets to stay with his mother and himself. As the group grew in size, they moved to a larger house. Today there are several thousand *muchachos* (boys) from the ages of six to twenty living in a town that is self-governing and self-supporting. The priest functions not as the authority, but as chaplain, friend, and adviser. The town is governed democratically, something of an anomaly in Franco's Spain. The members themselves take care of all their own needs. The community earns "foreign currency" through a traveling circus that bears the same name, and that was on tour in the United States in 1973.

The circus performers are trained by professional performers in Europe.[21]

Los Muchachos is, in fact, a fascinating experiment in community living, where children have what we normally think of as adult responsibilities. The children take their responsibilities very seriously, and the worst punishment that is ever meted out is expulsion from the community. Today, however, such a community would have to include girls. Perhaps this type of community provides an alternative for children who, for whatever reason, need to be out of their family situation.

A similar experiment designed as an educational experience was A. S. Neill's Summerhill in England. There the children took responsibility for their own learning and for the ongoing life of the community, but of course the community was much smaller than *Los Muchachos* and not self-supporting.[22]

5. The neighborhood form of community living is an attempt to build a sense of the extended family and of neighborliness that has too often broken down in the larger cities. An example is the Philadelphia Theological Community. This group considered itself primarily a vocational community, but also intended to be a support group. In this case, each member family had its own house or apartment, although there was some degree of economic sharing and a real concern to provide support for the individual family relationships. While it lasted, it provided a forum for ongoing discussion of educational, theological, and political questions, as well as room to experiment with new styles. This particular form of community may be more suitable at present, because it takes account of the fact that the American value system makes community living very difficult. All of us have internalized these values, even when we wish to live differently, and it takes time to build a new life-style.

REFLECTIONS

What people first discover about building community is that it takes time. There are few models for people choosing to live in a community to follow. But it is similar to marriage, in that people choose to live together, to work together, and to provide mutual support. Furthermore, there will be many forms of community living, and one may have to experiment to find the form that is suitable for the place, the time, and the people. A weekend spent together with some resource people can provide a time for common exploration and clarification of goals, both in fact and in imagination. The first stage will be to get some sort of feel for this kind of sharing and to set up limited goals. A further stage may be to begin some form of common ministry and common worship.

As the community begins to move, a variety of forms of group activity can be helpful at different stages. Resource people to illustrate processes like values clarification and conflict management can provide help for the community as it deals with inevitable disagreements and differences. Actually, conflict can help the people to clarify their own goals and to push the group ahead. It may also indicate that the group needs to re-form or regroup along different lines. Commitments to the group, therefore, would be made for a limited time, followed by a time of reevaluation.

CONCLUSION

The contemporary focus on alternative life-styles has given both young people and older people an awareness of the richness of human possibilities. This awareness of the variety of life-styles, work-styles, forms of community, and family is liberating and creative, though it may not always be easy for us if we have grown up with the idea that there is only one right way to live in a family.

Each of us has enough time and space to try out more than one option. Many people change professions in their middle years. Women have time to prepare for a whole new profession while their children are growing up.

The nuclear family, as we have seen, is intensive, close, and limited in emotional investment to the few members who make it up. At one end of the spectrum, personal loyalty is completed by these close relationships, and the individual feels no loyalty to persons or groups outside the family circle. This position is self-defeating: Families have no world to survive in when they are pitted against one another. The family can be as selfish, self-centered, and destructive to persons and groups as any individual can.

At the other end of the spectrum is the family that is completely open to the larger society. Such families are suggested in Plato's classic description of the ideal Republic, where women and children were part of the larger community.[23] Russia attempted such a utopian community, where the individual family was completely open to the public world. Similar styles were to be found in the Oneida community and among the Hutterites. At one extreme, the style may be one of low emotional intensity and, what one author has called in writing of the Israeli kibbutzim, a "flattening of personality." The point of alternate family structures is not that some are better for everyone, but that there are options available by combining private and public elements that help overcome the limits of the present nuclear family.

Where present nuclear family structures tend to be restrictive and exclusive, new communities can develop inclusive structures. Where present family patterns are unable to include single people and old people, new communal forms can provide place and time for warm and loving community. Older people no longer would have to depend on the dutiful love of married sons and daughters or the impersonal care of institutions; they could find scope for action in these communities. Maggie Kuhn commented once that the very fact of failing physical energy for older people was a plus, because cooperation was essential to accomplish things they once may have done alone.

Present information and experience of communal living suggests that it will require a learning process that most of us have not gone through in our youth. The constant input of several persons rather than one as in marriage can provide a threat to one's concept of reality. Personal problems may surface that would be hidden in other contexts. Initial ventures in communal living may need to be therapeutic, as may be the experience of marriage. Deconditioning from our total claims to another person's time is as necessary in the commune as it is in marriage, though in marriage, people are often expected to make such claims or to respond to them. If it is hard enough to accept one another in marriage, it may be vastly more difficult to accept several others in a commune. We may need to expect less from one another in order to accept one another as we are.

In short, it will take time to learn to live in an open community. When we become "deprivatized" with the help of a community, we learn to function better in larger groups, and can then take risks in the public sphere. Undoubtedly there will always be a tension between public concerns and private needs, but it is a tension and no longer a contradiction. The public sphere, too, can become a place of human concern, of development, and of growth toward our vision of shalom.

CHAPTER 5
WORK—TREADMILL OR CHALLENGE?

Work traditionally has been understood as punishment for Adam's sin, accomplished in sweat and tears. Hard labor can be part of a criminal sentence. Manual labor is considered the job of people low down on the socio-economic scale, and it is poorly paid. Technology has created machines to lighten the workload, but often at the price of enslaving people to machines on assembly lines or, worse still, of putting people out of work.

Work is a fact of life that for most of us is the central question of survival. We spend a good proportion of our lives working at our job or profession. In some sense our work becomes for us our identity, our class, and our worth in society. A person's work not only gives one identity, it defines one's communities. People describe themselves as engineer, teacher, housewife, even though these activities do not complete their identities, and they find their support communities among people in the same type of work. If we are to overcome the walls of hostility and build shalom, we cannot avoid communities of work.

These work communities may or may not be shalom communities. They may work for a vision of shalom or they may merely provide an income, or, as in the case of organized workers, become protection associations. To test what kind of communities they are, the following questions are useful: Do they help provide abundant life for all? Do they help liberate people? Do they seek peace and work publicly for it? Do they go the second mile for the poor? Do they act democratically?

In this chapter first we will name the problems of work. Second, we will analyze the values current work structures assume. Third, we will see how we can act to free work communities where we are and adopt alternative work structures that are available to us right now. Finally, we will start envisioning, freeing our imaginations to conceive new styles of work and to see how work itself can contribute to the building of a peaceable world.

NAMING THE PROBLEMS OF WORK

What are the chief problems of work today? Basically they are the following: (1) unemployment and underemployment, (2) inadequate pay, (3) dependency, in a master-servant relationship, (4) monotony, (5) high pressure, (6) lack of mobility, (7) compulsory retirement, and (8) discrimination against women in the labor market.

Unemployment and Underemployment

Unemployment in the United States is a *structural* or public problem rather than merely a private matter. That is, it is not temporary; it will not get better by itself as business picks up. Being unemployed is not necessarily something to blame an individual worker for. Rather, vast social forces beyond the control of individuals determine the availability of jobs. Unemployment will not be reduced significantly without profound changes in what we value and thus pay people to work. For instance, the massive unemployment of the Depression in the 1930s was resolved only with the coming of World War II. There is irony in the fact that we seem to need wars to assure full employment. Wars create demand for American-made guns, a demand that is never satisfied. The arms race and war itself continually use up American-made products so that nations always need more. We limit our production of food, housing, and public services, but apparently, we can never produce enough war materiel, at least according to the present priorities of the work structure. When concerned senators and others protest that millions of dollars have gone to Honeywell, Lockheed, or Boeing for military production, the effectiveness of the protest puts men (mostly men) out of jobs. *The workers literally can't afford to support peace.*

High unemployment levels mean that workers must find work where they can. Competition for jobs makes each worker the enemy of her brother (or his sister). Older workers are in an especially uncertain position; because when they are laid off, they often cannot find jobs comparable to the ones they held. This picture is not confined to blue-collar workers. There are high unemployment rates for white-collar workers, including middle management and upper management people. Unemployment also affects professionals, particularly teachers and engineers.

Obviously we need a new standard for determining productivity in our nation and what we value in work. By our present standards, weapons and other consumer products boost productivity while housing, new cities, food, and social services do not. Though public services are included in the reckoning of the Gross National Product, we do not really understand them as productivity. Our social priorities are dictated by money and profits, not by the shalom criteria of abundance, liberation, public peace, bias toward the poor, and democratic decision-making. As John Galbraith says: "In the general view it is privately produced production that is important, and that nearly alone. . . . At best public services are a necessary evil; at worst they are a malign tendency against which an alert community must exercise eternal vigilance." [1] As a result, we live with some odd contradictions. "Vacuum cleaners to insure clean houses are praiseworthy and essential in our standard of living. Street cleaners to insure clean streets are an unfortunate expense. Partly as a result, our houses are generally clean and our streets generally filthy." [2] Galbraith suggests that we do not value these things because they must be had publicly or not at all. They may not be viewed as productive because they do not belong to the business sector where profits are made. When our own criterion for production becomes: What will give abundant life for all? not: What will make profit for a few? then jobs will be as plentiful as is human need.

Inadequate Pay

Inadequate pay is a problem for both the poor and the middle class. The results are the same—a compulsion to continue working. For the poor, inadequate pay means that they work hard and still live at the poverty level. In order to survive, both parents must work and, if the family is large, the husband may need to take two jobs. Middle-class working people—teachers, secretaries, and executives—are trapped in a different way. They feel poor because they can never catch up with a continually rising standard of living. Credit buying leads many to live beyond their means. They must work to provide for the things they already have bought on credit. The future will take care of itself if our credit is good, but the past is like a wolf at our door. Once we get into this pattern, there is little freedom to change jobs, to try out something new. We find ourselves living at high anxiety levels, with the vision of a future that will be more of the same. It is a "Catch-22" society. The catch is that no matter how much you earn, it is never enough.[3]

Work as Dependence

If the threat of unemployment (or threat of nonadvancement) is the stick that beats the employee to work harder, the expectation of a rising standard of living is the carrot always dangled ahead as promise, yet forever unavailable.

Unions have helped some working people to organize and to demand higher wages, better working conditions, and better medical and retirement benefits. The unions, however, have also created two classes of workers. Unionized workers are a relatively select, secure, and privileged group. By far the greater number of workers are nonunionized and have no redress for grievances. The unions sometimes have functioned to keep women and minority groups out of well paid jobs, and in some cases have prevented the workers from forming their own unions.[4]

A time of high unemployment is a buyer's market. The demand for jobs is high, for people low, so that people must take what they can get. Many people must stick with jobs they hate because they cannot get other jobs. In such a situation, people find themselves trapped almost like indentured servants. By contrast, when employment is up, people have a greater sense of freedom and of opportunity. In either case people are dependent on forces beyond their control and dependent on decisions made by others over whom they have no influence. The job structure, contrary to the American dream of self-sufficiency, makes us vulnerable and dependent on powers beyond us. Liberation as one test of shalom is missing here.

Monotony

As long as a job provides new learning and a challenge, it can be pleasurable, at least to some degree. If it also brings personal recognition to the worker, the enjoyment is even greater. Where the job has been simplified and routinized in the interests of efficiency, it is quickly learned and accomplished by rote. It becomes mind-numbing and in the long run mind-destroying. The claim has even been made that mentally deficient people can do a better job on an assembly line than people of normal intelligence because they are less likely to rebel against monotonous work.[5]

Mechanized work subordinates human rhythms to machine rhythms. People become a mere extension of the machine. Auto workers on the assembly line, for example, are bound to the machine until the signal is given for the mid-morning break. In some cases, there isn't even time to go to the bathroom, and the workers are treated like children. Women in typing pools are treated the same way. I once found myself in an incredible situation: One hundred women were typing at their desks, working at an intense noise level, with no communication permitted with the other women workers until the whistle sounded for lunch. When the whistle sounded again, all the women quickly went back to work. The typing itself was on the worst assembly line principles. Four men were working also in that outfit, and (you've guessed it!) they were the executives, each with his own office. The men on the executive level had more freedom from monotony. They could come and go, chat in a leisurely fashion, and organize their own work.

Constant Pressure of Work

For some people in education there is the security of tenure, where they will not be laid off the job except for gross incompetence. Job security increases with high employment levels and decreases in times of unemployment. Academic freedom is felt to depend on tenure, but the same is true for any worker. Political freedom requires job security. Without some kind of job security, a worker cannot be expected to have anything other than a vested interest in his or her job. Job insecurity creates an enormous pressure to conform to the demands of the employer and to fear nonconformity in others.

Competitiveness is a second kind of pressure that exists in some jobs more than others. In the academic world one must publish more, be more popular with students, work faster, or work longer than one's associates.

Those who work at higher levels, and more independently, are not free from pressures either. Here the pressures take the oppressive form of work compulsion, turning these people into what some have called "workaholics." They are compulsive workers who cannot finish anything because they are perfectionists. For such people a simple, definite nine to five job would be a relief, because at least they could let the work go without constantly being worried about it.

However, "success" usually requires this kind of total commitment. Commitment to work is assumed even in our family structure. Male professionals often give generous praise to their wives for having borne the whole burden of the family while they devoted themselves to their first love, work.[6] This same dedication (compulsiveness) is given as a reason why women, who have no such "helpmate" to raise the family, cannot be as successful in their careers.

Lack of Mobility

Those who believe in the notion that upward mobility is possible find themselves caught also in the need for geographic mobility. In many cases advancement on the job requires moving to a different part of the country. While the man finds continuity in the job and the people with whom he works, his wife and children often find these moves very painful. For the worker, this mobility functions in such a way that all ties with the community outside the job are cut. His only ties are to the company.

If the wife is a professional in her own right, her job ordinarily gives way to his. She must leave her job to find another where he is, a job that necessarily will be secondary to his, both in terms of pay and of status.

The consequences of this mobility are serious. For the worker, dependence on his work and his employer may increase his separation from contacts outside the work context, while his family may find they are living in increasing social isolation.

Compulsory Retirement

If work is a burden as long as it lasts, forced retirement is also a burden, and also dehumanizing. The labor market demands a modern form of slavery. When people can no longer give their total energies, they are discarded. The present job structure often does not assume that older people have something to contribute to their society. For the man[7] who owns his own business or who is his own job master, the case is different. The economy permitting, he can work as long as he still has the desire and the energy.

Compulsory retirement functions to lay a heavy burden on workers in another way. For many it is a real struggle during the thirty to thirty-five years of working life to pay for one's debts as a student, to pay for one's children to receive a college education, and to provide sufficient income for retirement for oneself and one's spouse for another fifteen to twenty years beyond retirement age. As life expectancy increases, the proportion of retirement time will exceed working time. As it is, a working man who is the sole support of his wife and family must provide support for two children for twenty years, a wife for fifty to sixty years, and himself for fifteen to twenty years beyond retirement. He must work thirty-five years in order to provide 105 years in total support for his nonworking dependents, including himself after retirement. No wonder many men feel as if they need liberation more than women do! With increased life expectancy, traditional work and retirement patterns will have to change.

Discrimination Against Women in the Labor Market

There has been a job scarcity for women since 1945, when the "feminine mystique" [8] began to infect everyone. Prior to that time the acceptance of women in the labor market was greater even than today. After 1945, women were sold the idea of making housework and motherhood a full-time, totally satisfying occupation. The burden of earning a living fell totally on the men.

Recently women have been returning to the job market, either because of financial necessity, or because they feel the need to be part of the public world as they were before marriage. Yet women's work forms a different kind of slavery.

Usually housework is not considered to be work, because it is not paid. For example, it does not count for social security. The attempt is made to glorify housework and child rearing by calling it "homemaking," but domestics who do the same thing are very low on the socioeconomic scale. The glorification stops when it costs money. This work is the object of much TV advertising, which creates needs for many unnecessary consumer goods.[9] Advertising creates an image of the happy, though slow-witted, female who falls for the latest "miracle" soap pushed by the male huckster. Life circumscribed by the home can be a life deprived of social and intellectual stimulation.

Woman is a servant in the home, a responsibility she can escape only with difficulty, either because of her own or society's expectations. If she has a job, she feels pressured to say that her family comes first and to make sure that the house is always in order. Professional men are expected to put their work first. The contradiction in male and female roles can wreak havoc with the family.

Woman's status as servant carries over into her job outside the home. If she works in the office, she is usually secretary, servant, and office wife. She takes care of the menial aspects of the boss's work. She is the mediator with the outside world, so that his status is enhanced by his inaccessibility. She is often chosen because she is young and nubile, and many secretaries uncritically and unconsciously accept this image of themselves.

Job options for women have been limited. Women often are hired at the lowest levels as nurses, typists, sales girls, and factory women, with little hope of advancement. The rationale has been that they will get married and raise families and that, therefore, they are unreliable as workers. Studies, in fact, have shown that women are more reliable and have a lower rate of absenteeism than men. If women were given maternity leaves, their contribution in the work world would become increasingly important.

ANALYZING THE MEANING OF WORK

Oppressive as the work situation has often been, it nevertheless provides the worker with some sense of worth. Through one's work she or he can feel a part of the ongoing work of the larger society. Through work one is able to make a contribution to society. However, if one's personal identity is defined *wholly* by work and by getting ahead at work, one's life meaning is severely circumscribed and vulnerable to idolatrous forces.

Deeper than these personal problems is the question of *the public value of work*. For example, workers in a napalm factory have to work to live, and other jobs may not be available. How does one behave while holding a job that results in the production of weapons of war? If one feels responsible to speak out against these things, he or she risks unemployment. Within the past few years, prophetic Christians have started to ask such hard questions and have suggested alternatives. Both the question and the solution, however, will be ineffective if dealt with only at the individual level.

From a religious perspective, an individual's work is seen as a vocation and is a part of a larger calling. My life as a person is larger than my work, and the work of the community is broader than my individual work and contribution. Seen in a broader perspective of an individual's life and of the meaning of shalom community, a number of alternative types of work structure suggest themselves. If, for example, one looks at the total number of work years (thirty to thirty-five years), the nonworking years may be thirty-five to forty years, including the years of childhood and of retirement. It may make sense to divide the work so that instead of a forty-hour work week for a few years, people would have a thirty-hour work week for more years. Experiments with fewer work days—for example, a forty-hour work week of four days—have shown that work can be arranged differently. The work itself may remain the same, but it no longer requires all one's energies. Other alternatives become clearer in light of a vision of shalom.

ACTING TO CHANGE WORK STRUCTURES

Work structures are already beginning to undergo change, partly because young people, women, and Blacks coming to the work force have very different work values, and partly because the quality of work itself changes.

It may well be, however, that, unless we give some real thought to changing work values, we shall find ourselves enslaved by the grim necessities of Parkinson's Law. It says, in effect, that work always expands to fill all the time available. Automation and computerization may cut down on the necessity of the forty-hour work week, but they may also create more jobs, not because those jobs need doing, but because there is free-floating human energy available. This may be the psychology behind the increase of jobs relating to electronic surveillance, data gathering, and other questionable uses of technology. Because we *can* do it, somehow we *must* do it. The question is not being asked loudly enough—Do we need it? Should such work be done at all? Does it contribute to a vision of shalom?

In one way or another most of us get into a groove that leads into a particular job. Often we choose to do what parents or parents' friends do for a living. Or we take anything we can get that we are qualified for. Even well-educated people may not really have asked themselves some basic questions about work: If I had complete freedom to choose, what would I want to be or do? What needs doing in society that no one is yet doing? Then, with my gifts and talents, how can I begin to prepare for that kind of work? If no one is yet willing to pay for it, even though it is socially necessary, how can I begin to make that kind of work into a "doable action"? Can I work for money part-time and do what needs to be done in society on my own for a while? Below are some suggestions for creating more free space at work and, hopefully, some new work options.

Job Sharing

Women and younger workers today do not assume that work must absorb all their energies. Many would prefer part-time work, or job sharing. In some cases a husband and wife team or a group of friends could share a job. If every adult who wanted to work was guaranteed a job, the burden of support would not fall on the man as head of the family; and child rearing would not be the sole or chief responsibility of his wife. Also, with lighter work loads for everyone, there could be a guaranteed minimum income. Then, even the lowest paid job would pay a living wage.

If people wanted to work less in order to have more free time, this too would be possible. Guaranteed income and guaranteed jobs would take away the stigma of welfare. Cooperative day care centers would remove women from the isolation they have experienced in the care of small children. New work styles and altered work periods would then allow greater involvement of men with children.

Work as Learning Experience

Many people can make work a greater learning experience. Present job structures channel young people into certain jobs very early, so that the workings of society are a mystery to them. As part of their education, young persons should be able to spend a year as an apprentice in business, another in law, another as a paramedical aide, another in the Peace Corps—years in which they would be learning, working, and earning.[10] This concept of work as learning experience is an integral part of the educational process at Antioch College in Yellow Springs, Ohio, as well as at many seminaries.

Humanizing the Job

For those who are already working, there may be ways of humanizing the job. In Sweden, Volvo is changing from the assembly line of production to teams of workers who will produce a whole car together. For the team, there is a sense of shared work and of shared satisfaction on the job. The style is one of cooperation here rather than competition. In office work the same sense of teamwork could be developed, where the work is a common responsibility. Tasks could be rotated so that people have a sense of the whole.

In teaching school less emphasis might be placed on punitive discipline and more on learning in small groups, with adults working with children to open up new areas of discovery. Open classrooms and new learning styles are being tried in some American schools already.[11]

Changing Professions

Both men and women are discovering that they are dead-ending in their middle years. Women have raised children and are no longer professional mothers; men have gone as far as they can in a particular field. Both find themselves trapped. But the middle years can be for many a new beginning. For some, it will mean returning to school. Others may use their knowledge and experience to teach young people. Some may decide to leave the city to take up farming. Some women, building on their husband's help and prestige, are able to enter the commercial world and to take on responsible executive positions. One woman moved from taking care of her own house to managing a hotel. In her case, her husband was already a hotel manager.

What may be even more important is changing job descriptions in a time when companies are reorganizing. Women who were originally secretaries can rethink their own jobs, decide the direction in which they would like to move, and begin where they are or consider the possibility of a different job.

The change in professions or jobs is tied in with another fact that most of us have not yet taken full account of, the information explosion. Information has been doubling at a rate comparable to population. Information up to the year 1900 took only another fifty years to double, but at present it is doubling approximately every ten years. It no longer makes sense to go to school for the first sixteen or twenty years of one's life and to assume that one is prepared for the world. Life is, in fact, a continuous process of communication of discoveries, a process of learning and of the creation of new ideas and values. Working at a variety of jobs may itself be part of this learning experience.

Free-Lance Work

In this kind of job you can write your own job description. Many talents lend themselves to this sort of work—writing, art, music, research, photography. The problem is that it does not pay well, but it is the kind of work that a husband-wife team can take on if one of the two has a regular job. The free-lancer, for example, could do investigative reporting for a local newspaper or videotaping for a local television station. Several women have used parent effectiveness training as a kind of free-lance work. Many of these jobs require a great deal of ingenuity in getting to know people, and persistence in proving the ability to make a contribution.

ENVISIONING NEW WORK STRUCTURES

Many organizations, especially smaller ones, composed of younger people are able to move a step further in changing work structures themselves.

Democratizing Existing Structures

Here the attempt is made to give the workers a sense of participation in the overall work of the company. Profit sharing and first choice of shares in the company are a start. The invitation for suggestions and ideas from the workers is another. It is easier for the style of work and of policymaking to be egalitarian in smaller companies.[12]

Further democratization of the work process would lead to a sense of teamwork, especially among smaller work groups, a pattern appropriate to our vision of shalom. Some equalization of salaries has been tried, an arrangement that benefits younger and less skilled workers. The rationale here is that the work is cooperative and that each person's contribution is important. Where it has been tried, for example at Highlander Adult Education Center in Knoxville, Tennessee, it works because of people's commitment. The job itself is understood as intrinsically worth doing. One very large conglomerate company in Sweden, Granges AB, with 25,000 employees, is "breaking down power hierarchies and giving employees at all levels maximum decision-making power." This attempt at industrial democracy is a response to the young employees who "don't want a job they can learn in half an hour and just stand there moving their hands according to some fixed schedule," says Grange President, Johan Akermann.[13]

In the United States an insurance and brokerage firm called International Group Plans in Washington, D.C., is turning over 50 percent of the control to employees. The current owner, James P. Gibbons, is putting the stock into an employee-controlled trust for the purpose of "replacing business' traditional money-centered goals with . . . human-centered ones." [14]

These innovations are built on the principle that people can have a sense of personal worth, if they are in on the decisions that affect them.

Work Cooperatives

Here a group of people sensitive to community needs, as well as to the need for a new style of work, form cooperatives. The primary goal is service to the community, but also there is the need to make a living. The group may not even be averse to creating a surplus of capital—profit. The surplus in this case functions not so much as personal profit, but rather as money that can be made available for other community projects. Some possibilities are the following:

—*Craft Collectives* provide people with the option of using talents that have tended to get lost in an industrialized society. The purpose is to do what you want to do, to make enough to live on. Any profit goes to support community concerns, perhaps a credit union, which can finance low-cost housing or other cooperatives. In these cooperatives people have a different kind of freedom than in ordinary jobs and can often choose their own times to work, in recognition of the fact that work follows human rhythms if it is really expressive of the person.

—*Youth Screen Printing, Inc.* in Dayton, Ohio, was begun years ago as a center to train Black youth in silk-screen process.

Young people from ages eight to eighteen came to learn all stages of the process. Originally, the students learned every aspect of the business, including research and marketing. They even sat in on policy-making board meetings. Today the enterprise is too large for this kind of participation, and the business side has had to be separated from the screen printing. Youth Screen Printing, Inc., is now showing a profit, which is used to support the educational side of the enterprise, Youth Screen Printing Institute. For further information or for screen prints, write Mel Horton, Youth Screen Printing, Inc., 12 Ventura Street, Dayton, Ohio 45417.

—*The People's Garage* in Fayetteville, Arkansas, began when two young men came together to learn about repairing their own cars. As they gained expertise they were able to provide inexpensive and reliable service to their neighbors. The charge is reasonable for parts, with a modest $3.50 an hour for labor. To encourage other people to learn about their own cars, they provide the facilities of the shop for self-help, so that it is also a learning center that helps take the mystery out of car repair. This arrangement is a significant departure from the typical local garage. The People's Garage is also planning to have classes for women. A similar center is in operation in the Germantown area of Philadelphia.

—*Health Care* can be provided in the same way and already is in some cities. Some health centers are funded by the state, whereas others are financed by the community, where people pay on a sliding scale ahead of time. In this case, the venture requires considerable community support. Doctors who are concerned about community health are hired by the hour. Some centers also include mental health personnel.

Women's self-help centers are another socially beneficial alternative work. In these self-help centers, women learn how to give themselves Pap smears and also learn something about preventive medicine. These centers are usually run by women for women.

—*Alternative Schools* are springing up in every major city. In some cases they attempt to provide a freer learning situation than in traditional schools. For older children, programs like Philadelphia's Parkway program try to take the children out of the four walls of the school into the city, so that the city itself becomes a learning center.

In other alternative schools, community people are invited to teach some skill they have that others want. In these schools people of all ages mix, because education and learning are not confined to the young. In such situations the generation gap gives way to a common interest in learning something one has chosen to learn. To begin such a school as an alternative takes some doing, but by now there are people available who have a good deal of experience. Unless such schools can find support from a church or a foundation, however, they will not be accessible to people who are not affluent.

—*Public Interest Research Groups,* a large number of which have sprung up in the last few years, have gathered to provide socially valuable information to the public. Ralph Nader's groups come to mind. Here people accept subsistence salaries because the work is intrinsically worth doing. The corporate approach provides a profoundly different work style, one that gives people the satisfaction of knowing that their work furthers beneficial social change.

Public Discussion of the Issues

In addition to specific alternatives that individuals and small groups take on, there is the broader need for public discussion of the present work structure. So far, the only arena for discussion of goals and priorities in work exists in the universities, and at best discussion is limited there. Our approach to jobs tends to be short-range, pragmatic, and utilitarian. We set up jobs to produce cleaning product X, vehicle type Y, moon rocket Z, without really looking at the whole picture to see what needs doing in the United States and how those needs could be met. Churches concerned for shalom can well begin as centers for public discussion of priorities and as centers for community concerns.

Adult education classes are a natural arena for such discussion, beginning with people's perception of their own needs. Courses for women in law, creative arts, advertising, and auto repair are good starters.

CONCLUSION

Two contradictory trends are at war with each other today. On the one hand, we already have the technology to cut back the workload, to lighten the hardest work, to make working conditions safer and more humane. On the other hand are the increasing air, water, noise pollution and high pressured and monotonous working conditions that frenetic production creates. The cost of all this is paid most fully by low-income workers.

Whether the future will bring a greater equality in work and a greater sense of the worth of everyone's participation—or whether it will bring greater inequality with some workers doing all the dirty work of society—is a decision that can go by default or a decision that all of us can work at together. An individualistic, competition-oriented society belongs in the jungle; it is not a viable form for the complexity of the urban community. Our work community must embody a greater sense of shalom or it will not survive at all.

CHAPTER 6
THE MODERN CITY—BREAKDOWN, SHUTDOWN, OR SHALOM?

At the height of the layoffs at the Boeing factory in Seattle where unemployment ran at a high 15 percent, a billboard carried the message, "Would the last one to leave the city please turn off the lights?"

In pessimistic moments we may wonder what future the cities have. The city represents our most complex form of human community, but it appears that we may be left only with empty buildings, congestion, and chaos. People have moved out to the suburbs in an attempt to create a more human environment, only to discover that the problems have followed them. Crime (and theft in particular) is increasing in the suburbs. Moreover, the suburbs depend on the very cities that the people have left and rejected.

Up to this point in our consideration of shalom community, we have been discussing private communities identified in sex roles, work roles, marriage and family—aspects of community that touch us directly in a personal way. By contrast, the city is a public reality, a kind of giant that makes its own demands on us. The city is the place of big government, big business, big finance, big crime, big police systems, and, above all, big problems. To solve our personal problems, employment problems, family problems, legal problems, and health problems, we find a computer in some big city or a person trained to behave like one. We often feel we are being programmed negatively, and there is nothing to do about it but adapt. It is often easier to accept things as they are than to fight the giant institutions that control parts of our lives.

The city represents a style of life. It contains a concentration of affluence and power. The city is the end-result of a process in which wealth streams in from the countryside to be deposited in the deltas of the cities.

In biblical times the city was a mixed blessing. Cain, the murderer, is the founder of the city, and his descendants are adept at all the arts and technology that make the city a good place to live. David's struggle for kingship (at one time seen as a rebellion against God) included the establishment of the seat of government at Jerusalem, whose name means "God's shalom" or "God's peace." The city in history has inspired both hope and despair. Today in our cities, rotting and affluent neighborhoods exist side by side.

Many times, we feel our own powerlessness in the city. We make no difference to the life of the city. Many, if not most of us, choose to work and to buy in the city and to complain about it more as spectators than as participants in its everyday life.

Yet we need not be powerless. We can learn to flex our muscles, to make a difference in the city, in spite of its size and its indifference. What we need to do is to get at the root of our powerlessness and overcome the real walls of hostility in our cities. *My thesis is that the most basic problem is structured poverty*, or a rigid economic class system, which makes the city unfit for human habitation. Hand in hand with the problem of structured poverty is the philosophical assumption called individualism. We have tried in the past to build public community on the single motivation of private individual wealth. The results are the cities we have today, seemingly beyond personal control, especially the control of little people.

Let us begin letting our visions about city and the style it represents run wild. Then we will measure the dream against the reality—the problems of structured poverty and how the city has become the way it is. Last, we will reflect on what action we can take to create a city—old or new—that is pleasant for people to live in. A new city, of course, is not a new idea, but has been a dream of a broader, public community throughout the ages, a city of shalom.

ENVISIONING THE CITY

Dreams awaken us from the sleep of the everyday. They remind us of the possibility of hope for a new and more just society. But dreams also give power:

> The value of the utopian impulse lies . . . in its power to set men [i.e. people] free from their apathetic or suffering acceptance of the world as-it-is, and to give them self-transcending purposes.[1]

What would we wish in a city of shalom, a dream city, a city of the future, if we could get together and design it? What kind of relationships would we like to see between our work and our homes, between ourselves and our friends and all the good things that the city has to offer? How would we imagine a city where all the problems that we have come to associate with city living could be overcome—traffic jams, long commuting, inadequate parking, crime, pollution, slums, poverty and ugliness? What would men want from this future city? What would women want? What would children want? What would Black people want? What would white people want? What would Spanish-speaking people want? What would other ethnic groups want? Don't worry for the moment how it all fits together, but take time to imagine what the city could be.

Many of us would agree on the following:

—a city where everyone can walk down the street at night without fear.

—a city where there is clean air and blue skies, lots of trees, parks, and gardens.

—a city of pleasant streets, homes and shops.

But we also need some other things:

—a city with a fast and reliable transportation system.

—a city where walking is a pleasure, where pedestrian malls provide places to gather.

—a city that offers jobs which are not degrading to us as people and which pay enough to live on comfortably, where there is enough work for all.

—a city where women can make their contributions to the larger community.

—a city where children can learn with their friends and with adults other than their parents in places designed for children's purposes.

—a city where schools encourage creativity for children and plug into the life of the larger community.

—a city where our children can grow up, play, and go to school without fear.

Children want:

—a city that is not only for adults.

—a city of paths, parks, places to play and explore.

—a city where they are free to mingle with adults as they grow a little older; to participate in the adult world of work, art, and music; and to be respected for what they can do.

Much more could be added to a dream city, but I will leave it to you to complete the vision. Can we begin to create such a society now? What stands in our way as our society is presently set up?

To make dreams become a reality, Paulo Freire, like the prophets of the Bible, follows a double method. He denounces the negative aspects of the present situation.[2] Then follows the positive work of annunciation, of pointing out and of working toward the new vision.

In the past, concerned people, especially church people, have sought to make changes in the city merely by treating symptoms. Brigades of tutors, painters, nurses' aides, and volunteers of all kinds have come into the city to "help the poor." This made little difference because we never got to diagnosing the root disease—structured poverty—as a result of which the rich keep getting richer and the poor poorer. Until we understand this and begin to change it, helping the poor is only a patronizing diversion that keeps dreams of change from coming true.

The root problem of the city is more complex than the breakdown of family life or the fact of disorder. It is the more basic injustice of inequality and dependence. We need to examine critically the economic structure of the society we live in and to become aware of what Gustavo Gutierrez, a Peruvian Catholic theologian, describes as the "conflictual character of history."[3]

To recognize these conflicts is to recognize that the American dream in its first and naive stage is over. The second stage is to recognize evil, suffering, and injustice, and to make a renewed commitment as Christians to the work of building a new city of shalom.

ANALYZING STRUCTURED POVERTY

One of the most cherished aspects of our traditional American dream has been that of a society where all have an equal opportunity to become educated, to get a job, to work hard, and to succeed. We look at the achievements of this country with its advanced technology, based on hard work and intelligence. According to the myth, all of this is available to everyone who works hard. The fact of the matter is, however, that inequality is increasing everywhere. Our unexamined adherence to the myth hides the injustice of a highly structured economic system of interrelated economic communities, which we call classes.

In brief, we live in an unequal society, a class society. Economic inequality is not decreasing but increasing all over the world. This class society creates fear, suspicion, and isolation. Assistance to the poor, whether by welfare or charity, far from helping people to escape the cycle of poverty, gives them just enough help so that they can survive. By contrast, government benefits to the wealthy are abundantly available in the form of tax shelters, direct payments in farm subsidies, and government contracts. Let us look at these economic communities and how they work.

The Upper Class

A tiny percentage of Americans owns the majority of the nation's productive wealth.[4] This group is bound together not only by economic interest through the work that the men do, but also by social bonds cemented by the women as well as by intermarriage.[5] This class, unlike the middle and lower classes, also has a clear perception of itself as a distinct and distinguished community.

Not only does this group control most of the wealth, it also exercises political power. William Domhoff, one of the few scholars to do research on the upper class, defines this group of people as "active, working members of the upper class and high-level employees in institutions controlled by members of the upper class." [6] Their exercise of power exists "to maintain and manage a socio-economic system which is organized in such a way that it yields an amazing proportion of its wealth to a miniscule upper class of big businessmen and their descendants." [7]

The men who compose the power elite contribute heavily to both political parties. Because they contribute impartially, they exercise power beyond the party system. Government exists to further their goals. Much of their activity is exercised behind the scenes, hidden from the public eye. Their influence is all the greater because it is secret.

It is not surprising that this class controls most of the nation's wealth. The top fifth of the income bracket receives nearly 44 percent of the nation's combined income, whereas the bottom fifth receives only 3.7 percent.

The rationale of our economic system is to give incentives to the rich because their money is needed for investment purposes. If they invest in production, their investment will increase the Gross National Product (GNP), so that there will be a bigger pie for everyone to have a slice. Eventually, according to the theory, this wealth will "trickle down," and there will be enough for even the poorest to live well. In the meantime, stopgap measures like welfare and unemployment insurance are supposed to take the edge off the worst economic suffering. For the old, social security provides a minimal standard of living. But in the meantime, the poor get poorer, because the trickle-down theory is a myth and an opiate; it simply does not work.

These incentives to the rich come out of your pocket and mine in many ways. We mistakenly complain about the money we spend on welfare for the poor. The amount that is spent on "welfare" in the form of tax write-offs for the rich is considerably larger than the amount of welfare spent on the poor. Concessions to the wealthy cost more than $40 billion a year in lost taxes, whereas welfare for the poor costs a mere $4.5 billion,[8] more than paid for by the $6 billion a year taken in *taxes from people below the poverty level.*

One of the most obvious benefits to the rich is in the form of farm subsidies, originally meant to "encourage, promote and strengthen the family farm." But in fact, most of this welfare goes to large commercial farms, "agribusiness." Since the start of the program, $90 billion has gone to agribusiness; in 1967 alone the total was over $14 million. In one year, Senator James Eastland received $146,000 in farm subsidies for not growing cotton.[9]

The theory of farm subsidies has been that by keeping food prices high, the small farmer can make a decent living. In fact, however, the benefits have been disproportionately in favor of the large landowners. We the consumers have paid twice—once for the subsidy itself and once again for the honor of buying higher priced food in the supermarket.

The rich have other benefits. No income tax at all is paid on municipal bonds. Their yield may be as high as 6 percent, but their real value is considerably higher because they are not taxable. Income from capital gains is taxed at only 25 percent of its value at the time a sale is made, compared to the tax on earned income. This too is a tax scheme that benefits the wealthy, because ordinary people are not likely to have much capital gain. Even the 5 or 6 percent of bank interest is taxed at the same rate as earned income. J. Paul Getty, the oil millionaire, one of the wealthiest men in the world with a reputed income of $300,000 *per day*, paid only a few thousand dollars in income tax in the early sixties. In 1970, 1300 people with incomes of more than $50,000 paid no federal income tax at all.[10]

Corporations do not pay their fair share in taxes. The hundred largest corporations in the United States paid 27 percent of their income in federal taxes compared to the average small business, which pays 44 percent. The contribution of the corporations to federal taxes has gone down from 23 percent to 18 percent in the last ten years. By contrast, the share coming from payroll taxes has gone up from 19 percent to 30 percent.[11] Furthermore, the corporations treat this tax as an additional cost to be passed on to the consumer so that again the consumer pays extra.

Sales taxes and city and state income taxes are regressive when they take a straight percentage of income, because they take a proportionately larger bite out of the incomes of the middle and lower income wage earner. As a result they benefit the rich rather than the poor.

Corporations receive more diréct forms of welfare than the poor. One has only to think of the bailout of Lockheed by the government in 1972 or of the government investment of $1.7 million in Gap Instrument Corporation stock, a company with whom the Navy has a contract. It is a case of corporate socialism for the rich in this country and competitive capitalism for the smaller wage earner.

Giant corporations seldom compete for the military markets. Rather it is the poor and middle income employee who competes for everything he or she gets. The government gives tax money away to huge corporations and lets the rich thrive on tax loopholes, while the little people pay the bills.

One of the reasons this structured wealth continues is that people with little money vicariously identify themselves with wealthy people. The average person naturally wants to be rich, too, and hopes to imitate those who are. This hope is reinforced with each pay raise and with each new level of consumption. We are able to identify with the rich because we feel our own standard of living rises little by little every year. What is hidden is that this group has effective control of wealth and power. In many areas, we have lost power over our lives, our cities, and our life-styles. This lack of power is hidden by the fact that we do not question the economic structure. Those who do question the system, or work for reform and justice, begin to know what the powerlessness of the ordinary citizen is.

The Middle Class

The economic community in the middle includes all those who work for a living and who receive wages of any kind. Some professionals—notably doctors, lawyers, upper level executives, and college professors who contract for research and consultation to government and industry—form an upper middle class of substantial privilege. These people or their children can marry into the upper class. Marriage has always provided a form of upward mobility for the talented few.

The middle middle class is a large group where most of us are struggling to make payments on our rising standard of living. Today, the upward mobility of this class exists primarily at the consumer level where we attempt to imitate the rich. But the interests of the very rich and the moderately rich are not our interests. Our taxes benefit them at our own expense.

The fact that we imitate the rich conceals the reality that there are very oppressive elements in our lives. We live, as they do not, with basic insecurities of job uncertainty or major illness that can wipe out savings. The demands of a rising standard of living to which we can never measure up continue to bind us to a treadmill of work. In some sense, we have much to gain if we make common cause with the poor. Perhaps social change toward a more humane economic and political system would happen if we saw the structure as it really is. At present, we can make more in dollars every year. But we may not be better off in real earnings or in an improvement in the quality of human life.

The Working Poor and the Welfare Poor

These are people who are underemployed or unemployed, or who live in poor rural areas. Some of them do not have even enough to eat.[12]

What characterizes poverty, above all, is unemployment both over the long and short run. When people are unemployed over a long period of time, they begin to understand what it means to be poor. Unemployed professional people begin to feel like poor people. They begin to doubt themselves and their own capacities and if they go for a long time without adequate employment, they may suffer a real loss of identity.

The structure of our economic communities makes those whom it oppresses most feel guilty for that oppression. In our society, worth is tied up with a job; employment is both a *condition* of worth and a *consequence* of worth. But this is a vicious circle. Middle-class people cannot identify with the poor, because by definition they have worth and the poor do not (that is, on the competitive value scale). But until we do look at the situation that punishes some of its citizens by condemning them to live at the bottom of the American ladder of success, and see how that same system is also punishing the middle class, we will be unable to make changes. To the extent that people feel personally guilty and inadequate, they dare not share their problems with others. They are isolated and made powerless.

Originally intended to provide aid to those unable to work, unemployment insurance provides just enough to survive. In many ways, welfare has overtones of certain practices of charity, whereby people felt obliged to help the poor enough to salve their consciences but not enough to make the poor independent. Expenditures are minimal. As already mentioned, the government in 1970 actually collected $6 billion in taxes from poor families with incomes of less than $4,000 (that is, income below the poverty level) and paid out $4.5 billion in welfare benefits.

Welfare payments provide no more than a bare minimum for recipients. For example, in January 1972, the average payment for each recipient was $52 per month under the Aid to Families with Dependent Children (AFDC) program. This program accounts for 72 percent of all welfare payments. Most of the rest are to blind, disabled, or old people—a far cry from the myth of welfare chiselers who refuse to work and who drive Cadillacs at public expense. For a mother on AFDC with three children, the average income is $197 per month or about $2,400 per year. The image many of us have—that families are perpetually on welfare—is not borne out by the figures. In 1971, 68 percent of AFDC families were on welfare for the first time, and the average length of time that they had received AFDC was less than two years. Only 6 percent had received welfare more than ten years.[13]

The problem is not only jobs but also income earned by working. Poverty is defined as an income of $4,500 or less for a family of four, a figure that has not been changed in some seven or eight years, in spite of a continuing inflationary spiral.

Women are especially hurt by the welfare system. For example, one program called the Work Incentive Program (WIN) amounts to involuntary servitude by threatening to take away welfare altogether if the woman does not work. If she does work, under the current AFDC program, a portion of her earned income is subtracted from the welfare payment.[14] Thus, the program effectively insures that a woman stays at the poverty level and gives her no incentives, no help for getting an education in order to take a better job or for providing an education for her children. In addition, day care centers, which can make it possible for welfare mothers and other mothers to work, were vetoed by the same president who was concerned that people on welfare get on "workfare." The long-range view shows that investment in children and in people educated enough *to make a difference* would "pay off" the society far more than investment in buildings, factories, or the defense industry.

What the existing welfare structure reveals is our own ambivalent attitudes about work. We assume the poor do not want to work because work is unpleasant. A recent study has shown, however, that welfare does not reduce the incentive to work.[15]

If the poor themselves realize that life can be better and if they begin to make demands on society—as the rest of us have—through unions, through economic boycotts and the like, then the situation could become explosive. Why can there not be a union of poor people, an organized community of common interest, demanding jobs that pay decently? Why can there not be unions of poor and middle-income people demanding better housing, and unions of women demanding child care? The Welfare Rights Organization is a good start in this direction. But today we can go further. Unions of unemployed people (including unemployed professionals and teachers) can redesign job descriptions according to the way they see society using their talents and training today.

We lack these kinds of unions in part because we all fear poverty and mistakenly tend to identify our interests with the community of the wealthy and privileged. We are isolated from one another in our struggle for upward mobility. There is no organized, self-conscious community based on economic concerns. This is part of the reason that we can be exploited. If we are unemployed professionals, or just unemployed workers, we punish ourselves, are ashamed, and doubt our own self-worth. We blame ourselves or the poor for what is structured poverty. The last thing we want to do is make our poverty public. But when we learn that it is the result of a rigged system rather than our laziness, then we will protest. Women especially tend not to have a sense of self-worth on the job market and prefer jobs where the possibility of failure is less.

Costs of the American Class System

If the city, our public community, breaks down, it is basically an economic problem whereby the rich profit and the poor and middle income people fight each other for the few benefits that are left. The result is the chaos of individualism, noncommunity and antishalom in our cities. Cities provide many of us with a fair degree of comfort, and, what is more important, there is the constant promise of *more*. The comfort and fascination with money and what money can buy, the freedom that money seems to give, all *hide from us the human costs of this system*. Increasingly, however, these human costs are paid for not only by the expendable[16] people of our society—the young, the old, the poor, the hard-core unemployables, the returned veterans, the sick, the dying—all of us must pay these human costs in the form of pollution, unsafe streets, overcrowded highways, increasing unemployment, war, hunger, unsanitary housing and, worst of all, the spiritual cost of the loss of hope.

What are these basic social costs of the economic class system? They include, first, social dislocation and alienation; second, the mutilation of human beings both physically and spiritually; third, the destruction of the environment; and fourth, the continuing existence of poverty, the basic problem of our decadent cities, the public communities of antishalom.

It is hard to convince people that poverty and economic classes exist because we are given the wrong criterion by which to measure them. The Gross National Product (GNP) is the rule for measuring our wealth in quantitative terms. But this criterion does not measure the social costs of poverty. There are alternatives. For example, economist and Nobel prizewinner Paul Samuelson suggests a qualitative index of productivity, which he calls "Net Economic Welfare." Unlike the GNP, which includes both the production of pollution and the cost of cleaning it up as productivity, Samuelson's measurement would subtract these social costs as costs. Although he admits that this gauge is still very primitive, it is better, he says, "to have an inaccurate sense of what we want than an accurate sense of what we do not want."[17]

Besides changing our economic criteria, it is important to go deeper into the problem of poverty and the breakdown of the public community, the city. Poverty exists because there is little or no community among the people who have to get together to wipe out poverty and build public community.

Because the cities are basically a form of public community that exists for the mutual benefit of their inhabitants, the solutions to making better cities will come when they are reformed along the lines and for the purposes of economic change. In the past, individual initiative provided us with the spiritual drive to build massive structures and amass large quantities of goods. Now we need a community motivation that will drive us to undergird our common life with qualitative goods. These goods do not have built-in obsolescence; they do not wear out or need to be replaced with next year's model. Like good wine, qualitative goods grow richer with age. For Christians, the criteria of well-being can be found in an old book called the Bible. Well-being is another word for shalom.

ACTING TO BUILD A NEW CITY

A Theology of Poverty

In the Old Testament, God through the prophets is biased toward the poor and weak. He protects the needy (Psalm 109:31) and is against those who oppress the poor (Amos 4:1–2). He executes justice for the oppressed and gives food to the hungry (Psalm 146:7).

In the New Testament, God puts down the mighty, exalts the lowly, and feeds the hungry with good things (Luke 1:52–53). Before the multitude, Jesus blesses the poor (Luke 6:20). He seeks abundant life for them as well as their liberation. Jesus reaffirms the prophetic insight into God's love for the poor and oppressed.

Gustavo Gutierrez, theologian of liberation already referred to, points out that poverty is a situation of slavery and of sin, but the blame for it is now placed on the victim. As Moses led his people out of Egypt, Jesus leads his people not only out of personal sin, but out of the situation of evil and of oppression into freedom.[18] To know God is to do justice. Christians who use Jesus' saying, "You always have the poor with you" as if it were a prediction have misunderstood both the Old and the New Testament on the meaning of poverty.

Doing shalom is sharing with Jesus in the liberating work of overcoming the walls of hostility. But it is also a work of new creation, building a shalom world. In summary, Christians are once again called to shalom, defined as abundance for all, liberation of the oppressed, public as well as private peace, a bias toward the poor, and a free choice to control one's life.

Becoming a Ministering Community

SUPPORT ACTION

The Gospel is not only something to be studied, known, and tasted. It is something to be acted and lived out. If we are to build shalom in our cities, then we must become more and more active in community. We are not called to live as individual Christians in the world. The privatization of religion in the past has had the effect of a policy of "divide and conquer." The influence of Christians on society has been diminished when they have thought of social concerns primarily on an individual level. Ministry today must be not only a public ministry, but even a political ministry, opening structures up to the full development of the less privileged.

Churches can form strong core groups to operate as action groups. They can sponsor a few individuals and support them in action projects. Or they can commit themselves to various forms of action as a group. Such action groups, for example, can take on their own neighborhood. The neighborhood group can take on community problems such as the condition and supply of low and middle income housing. They can take further action as a group, perhaps working with other groups, to make their views known on policies concerning the city as a whole. They can also send money directly to groups of people working on social action projects in the cities.

For example, in Alabama a group that calls itself the LINK Society aims to create ties between the two thousand inmates of Atmore State Prison and their families. They have applied for funds and have received $35,000 from the Catholic Campaign for Human Development. Their basic goals are (1) getting families together, (2) providing legal aid, and (3) providing health care.[19]

POLITICAL ACTION

Political action groups must raise public issues to consciousness. They must also demand better reporting on these issues and insist on the necessary information to carry on public discussion. Some of the issues that need discussion are the question of national priorities, increased participation in power at the local level, defense spending, guaranteed employment for everyone, a minimum wage, fair taxes, and peace spending (as opposed to military aid) in poor countries.

A political action group may begin as a public affairs group. One of the difficulties in this approach, however, is that we soon develop a sense of our own powerlessness and inability to act. In part, this has to do with the nature of indefinite talk. Once we are comfortably ensconced in a living room with our friends, action seems to become less and less possible. A public affairs group must be an active group. Action itself can provide new sources of energy, a sense of power.

If the initial analysis is correct, we need to establish intermediate groups between big government, or even city government, and individuals and their families. These groups could give the individual a sense of power, a sense of working on some social issues together with others. There are already many such organizations, a few of which are described below.

Common Cause is a partisan citizen group. It works as a lobby on issues such as the responsiveness of Congress to the people, and is presently concerned about the question of seniority on congressional committees, the Equal Rights Amendment, and pollution. It placed pressure on the President and on Congress to end the war. It has a central organization, which you can support by donating money (not tax-deductible). It is also concerned with building grass-roots organizations, where people can work on local situations with the help of resources at the national level. Address: Common Cause, 2030 M Street, N.W., Washington, D.C. 20036.

Public Citizen, Ralph Nader's group, functions in a similar way, except that Nader is concerned more specifically about the quality of consumer goods and work safety. His persistence in researching automobile manufacturing has resulted in revolutionary changes with regard to auto safety standards, and his research on the interests of members of Congress has been another milestone. Older people are working with Nader on the special problems of senior citizens, such as nursing homes. Professionals are offering their services for a subsistence salary in order to do what they think is socially necessary. Address: Public Citizen, Inc., 1346 Connecticut Avenue, N.W., Washington, D.C. 20036.

National Organization for Women (NOW) is a moderate group that works on problems of discrimination against women in jobs and in public life. Members of NOW have done studies on children's books and school readers to show how little girls and women have been pictured as subordinate and dependent at every level. They are also working on paid maternity leaves and the revision of welfare laws to provide dignity for poor women. Address: National Organization for Women, 1957 E. 73rd Street, Chicago, Illinois 60649.

National Urban Coalition has developed the publication *Counterbudget: A Blueprint for Changing National Priorities (1971–1976),* edited by Robert S. Benson and Harold Wolman for the National Urban Coalition (New York: Praeger Publishers, 1971, $2.95). This group stimulates discussion and action across the nation on the use of the tax dollar. Formation of local groups is welcomed. Address: National Urban Coalition, 2030 M Street, N.W., Washington, D.C. 20036.

Tax Action Campaign needs help to work on tax reform. Work to be done includes circulation of petitions insisting on fair taxes, finding out what the facts are, and getting others to act. Also important is writing letters to your congressperson. Address: Tax Action Campaign, 1921 Pennsylvania Avenue, N.W., Washington, D.C. 20006 (Fred A. Harris, Chairperson).

THEOLOGICAL/POLITICAL ACTION

Create a forum for the discussion of public issues as they relate to people's wishes, hopes for the future, and the vision of shalom. This may be another way of developing the kind of discussion mentioned in the previous section. But such discussion/reflection/action goes beyond immediate issues to the larger human context. One such method of group process is the method of *conscientization*, as suggested in Chapter 2.

PROPHETIC ACTION

In the Old Testament, the prophets frequently used symbolic action to show, not just to speak of, the new reality. Sometimes it was fasting; sometimes it was a pointing to something that already existed, but which became a sign.

—Try living on a welfare budget with your family. Get your church to announce this action for a week and invite other families to participate. Check with your local welfare office for the amount allotted for food per person per week. June Rossbach Bingham, who did it, wrote up her experiences:

> The tastelessness and monotony of the goods available on welfare became depressing even though we were on it merely for one week. . . . The main trouble with a diet made up mostly of starch is that one is subject to flash-hungers between meals. Without warning, one is not merely hungry; one is ravenous, hurting, unable to concentrate on anything except getting something into the stomach.

Further on she says,

> During the latter half of the week, despite added quantities of oatmeal for breakfast, I found myself frequently empty, as against consciously hungry, and too lethargic to force myself to the typewriter. . . . Accompanying the loss of concentration was a loss of physical energy. . . . [How] can people be expected to get off welfare when they cannot afford to buy the proteins and vitamins, the so-called "brain foods that energize?" [20]

With this kind of symbolic action as a start, work at such projects as developing less degrading types of family assistance than those presently existing, establishing day care centers, and enforcing or increasing minimum wage standards. Above all, as Christians, we need to be concerned about poverty and inequality *on a structural level.*

—Build caring communities. Most of the action already suggested has been designed not for individuals, but for groups—action that also develops a sense of community. As the work goes on, it is important to remember that the people who are working are also people who have personal needs. Otherwise, these communities of concern can become as impersonal and uncaring as many business organizations.

Young people's efforts to build communal living situations may not be too different. Communal living also has a long and venerable tradition. What is often cited as the high failure rate of communes may only mean that it takes us a very long time to learn how to live together in larger groups.[21]

New City Models

New cities that are designed and planned from the beginning are an important alternative. It is not enough to patch up old structures. Today we need people who can experiment and develop new and more humane structures. This building of communities from nothing is in the best American tradition.

Columbia, Maryland, is one of the best known and most successful. A single developer planned it to be a city rather than a suburb, combining work places, shops, and civic centers as well as houses. There is a racial and economic mix in the city. Because many of the people came to Columbia precisely because of its aims, the population has to some extent been self-selected.

The city itself is built up of neighborhoods that have their own churches, schools, and community centers. On the larger level, in the center city, there are civic centers, large shopping centers, and art museums. At the neighborhood level, there are town meetings to decide policy; and although there are usually not too many people at these meetings, they are nonetheless an important part of the town's life.

Church groups have sponsored low and middle income housing in Columbia. So far they have been able to provide thirty-three subsidized housing units. A handsome four-bedroom town house costs $151.50 per month, and is just as well-designed, just as attractive, as any other town house in Columbia. The philosophy here is that the poor must be helped to become part of the community, not shoved into a welfare status that demeans them and angers the community. But Columbia is not the perfect city either. Only 15 percent of its residents actually work in the city, so that it still is more like a suburb than a city. Many values reflecting the separation of suburb from city are still very much in force, but it is at least a beginning.[22]

So far, cities like Columbia, Maryland, have been worked out by forward-looking developers who have taken the risks because they thought the profits were worth it. Government has not gotten into the act, because of the nation's fear of government planning. The time is ripe for public discussion of new cities. Such discussion can begin by having city planning and development courses for adult groups, studies of city problems, possible solutions, and new alternatives. Instead of focusing on training a select few in the graduate schools who will be the planners for the rest of us, information should be made available for people themselves to decide what sort of cities they want to live in. Then people can begin to plan and build cities with very different patterns. Cities need not be the same, but can have an enormous amount of variety.

One such effort to involve people in the actual planning and cooperative financing of a new city is the *Pahana Town Forum* in California, where a group of people is attempting to build a town that will take account of its ecology, a town of many parks and no cars. The aim is to have a face-to-face community, where people can live together. The town itself will be an environment for a different style of work, an attempt to live at a slower pace, to achieve some things in community.

The planners foresee an optimal size of 2,500, which would allow for government by the people at town meetings. Public education would be of the free school variety, with the whole city becoming a part of the learning environment. For further information, write: Pahana Town Forum, 629 State Street, Santa Barbara, California 93101.

The Pahana experiment is new in that it takes up contemporary concerns, but its approach is very old both in the Catholic and the Protestant traditions. In the fifth century, St. Benedict and his followers attempted something similar by clearing and filling swamps and then building new towns. The monks, who formed the core of the new towns at the beginning, were followed by families who came to settle this new area. The monastery existed for the community, and the monks taught people how to farm their lands more effectively, how to grow new foods, and how to celebrate on Sundays and holy days. A similar Protestant group was the Bruderhof, who formed in effect small self-contained towns.

CONCLUSION

Today's cities represent gross inequality, as well as lack of community. Individualism and poverty have turned sections of our cities into jungles, with affluent high-rise buildings in the midst of ugly and deteriorating neighborhoods. We can either continue as we are, pursuing our own private good, or we can begin building bridges to one another, which means "deconditioning" ourselves from the old life of competitive values, and adopting a new life-style of caring and sharing. Here as Christians we have some special resources—a long tradition of community, as well as some present experience of a caring community. Even where churches fall short, they still exist as a reminder of the promise of community. This new life-style of caring and sharing raises many questions, as we have seen. Already we have looked at problems of work, of sex roles, of marriage, and of social life in cities. The next question that we need to take up is that of global shalom.

CHAPTER 7
THE GLOBAL VILLAGE—WHOLENESS OR HOLOCAUST?

The world we are living in is becoming smaller and increasingly interdependent. Marshall McLuhan says we are living in a "global village." Old barriers of national boundaries and languages are giving way. Anything that happens in one part of the globe can be seen on television in other parts. The quest for shalom community on a worldwide scale today takes on new dimensions and new urgency.

At one stage, shalom in the Old Testament meant security and well-being only in a small village or nomadic tribe. The tribe often would go to war with another tribe paradoxically to establish peace or shalom for itself. Although nations still "kill for peace," the biblical concept of shalom grew from this early notion of tribal shalom to shalom within a confederation of tribes under Joshua, and then to a view of shalom as national peace and security under David. After the failure to obtain shalom under the kings—that is during and after Israel's defeat and captivity—the prophets' notion of shalom expanded further to include the whole world. In the New Testament, shalom is projected both as a vision for all people—Jew and Gentile, male and female, slave and free—and as a vision for the whole cosmos.

Unfortunately, the operative meaning of peace in the world today still reflects the period of national sovereignty in which people follow the king in "killing for peace." If we are to be guided by a vision of shalom broader than this limited view, it is necessary to develop a new approach to our "global village." We will need to seek shalom beyond the limits of our families, tribes, and nations. Global shalom is our goal.

RIGHTLY NAMING VIOLENCE

So far in this book we have sought shalom by overcoming the walls of hostility in our sex roles, our competitive work, and family lives, and in the public community of the city. The method guiding us has been inspired by the South American, Paulo Freire, who teaches a process (presented in Chapter 2) that helps us get handles on the structural, social origins of our walls of hostility—our noncommunity.

Now we return to South America to look briefly at some antishalom aspects there. It serves as an example of the whole Third World, of the vast walls that must be overcome. South America is particularly critical to us North Americans because it is so close to us. Some people take it for granted as one of those "free world" regions of Juan Valdez, Carmen Miranda, and "Banana Republics," which come under the U.S. protection of the Monroe Doctrine and the Alliance for Progress.

With this popular notion of a benign, simple people happily living under our tutelage, it is not surprising that the church's approach has been one of simple charity and help to the less fortunate. However, Freire and many other South American theologians insist that they do not need this kind of help, that this kind of helping hand is smothering them. Instead, they can help us gain a positive perspective for a new approach to seeking shalom on a global scale.

ANALYZING COVERT VIOLENCE

Basic to this new perspective is the wall of hostility called "covert violence." This violence—the result of unjust structures, policies, and trade agreements—keeps people hungry, ill, and enslaved. It escapes the headlines and TV screens, but its effects are as bad and often worse than the overt violence of war. The structured violence of poverty, hunger, and powerlessness affects many generations of people whom the wealthy assume are lazy, born inferior, or careless about *mañana.*

We must change our perspective! Because we have modernized and industrialized in the West, it is easy to assume that South America should do so too. We take it for granted that our own history provides the only model for development of poorer countries. But the economist of development, Robert Theobald, points out that the problems of these countries go beyond any models that we presently have of capitalism or communism. He points out that "these areas face a problem unique in human history. . . . The cold war has become an anachronism in the age of the hydrogen bomb; either the world survives together or it will blow itself to pieces." [1]

We will look briefly at some aspects of covert violence—poverty, hunger, and powerlessness—and we will look at them free of the notion that Western technology is the only answer to alleviating them.

The Current Distribution of Wealth

With its 210 million population, the United States accounts for only 6 percent of the world's population, although we consume 35 percent of the world's resources. When we include the other wealthy countries of the world (Western Europe, Canada and Australia), the figures become more extreme. Only 20 percent of the world's population controls 80 percent of the world's wealth. The Gross World Product is $3 trillion, an average of $1,000 for every man, woman and child in the world today. More than $1 trillion is produced by the United States alone. Another $1 trillion is produced by the industrial nations of Europe plus Canada and Japan. Another $1 trillion is produced by Russia, East Europe, China, and all the developing nations of Africa, Asia, and Latin America. Together Western Europe and the United States form an international upper class that controls two-thirds of the world's wealth.

This does not mean that the developing nations are not growing. They are, and their growth rates often exceed those of the United States. Yet as fast as they grow, the affluent nations advance more, in real dollars, so that the gap increases every year. For every advance that the poor countries make, says Barbara Ward, "the fully developed nations make a hundred more. The gap increases because they move at the speed of a bicycle, [while] their wealthy neighbors [move] at the speed of a moon rocket." [2]

Note these statistics on the wealth of the world and where it is concentrated.

Gross National Product and Population[3]

Country	Year	GNP Per Capita (U.S. Dollars)	Population (millions)	Growth Rate (percent)
A. Very Poor Countries (less than $100 per capita)				
China	1965	86	716.2	1.8
India	1965	88	494.6	2.5
Nigeria	1965	78	59.8	3.8
B. Poor Countries ($100–$249 per capita)				
Brazil	1965	224	83.8	2.9
Rhodesia	1965	221	4.4	2.2
C. Middle Income Countries ($250–$749 per capita)				
Chile	1965	484	8.8	2.5
Colombia	1965	262	18.3	2.9

Cuba	1965	329	7.7	2.0
Yugoslavia	1965	468	19.7	1.1
D. Rich Countries ($750 and up)				
Argentina	1965	764	23.2	1.6
Canada	1965	2100	20.2	1.9
Kuwait	1965	3272	0.4	4.8
Norway	1965	1618	3.8	0.9
United Kingdom	1965	1550	54.2	0.4
United States	1965	3240	196.9	1.3
U.S.S.R.	1965	1000	232.3	1.3

In this inequality, there is a double contradiction. The wealthy countries produce surpluses that remain in the wealthy countries. The wealth that is developed from Venezuelan oil, and Bolivian tin does not remain in these countries, but goes to the United States and other countries investing in South America. Some economists estimate that for every dollar of foreign investment, there is a return of two dollars to the United States.

Furthermore, foreign aid to poor countries comes with many strings attached. First, aid that is designated for arms and for heavy machinery for factories and farms must be spent in the United States. Most aid money is not sent abroad but goes directly to U.S. companies who then ship the goods. Second, prices for these goods are considerably higher in the United States than in Japan or Western Europe. Third, these purchases are required to travel in American ships. Fourth, after a number of years, interest payments accumulate, and new loans with more interest have to be taken out to cover previous loans and interest. Unlike the Marshall Plan, which gave some 80 percent of aid to Europe in the form of grants, aid to Latin America takes the form of loans with interest.[4] In effect, Latin American countries have mortgaged their futures, not for the benefit of the people, but to maintain small ruling elites in power. U.S. aid then becomes a subsidy payment to U.S. manufacturers, shippers, and exporters. What our benevolent aid program means is that our taxes pay U.S. companies to ship goods to the rulers of Third World countries, who may or may not deliver them to the people. Most of these goods will stay with the rulers because about half of the aid at the present time is for military and police assistance.

The Violent Results of Poverty

In Latin America, poverty is so chronic that it kills more people than does war. Hunger stunts growth, creates a condition of continuous ill health and low energy levels, and finally kills people off at the age of thirty or forty. Increasing poverty tends to be absorbed. Gary MacEoin, a journalist who has studied Latin America for twenty-five years, reports that peasants who used to be able to grow vegetables on a little plot of land around their shacks today have the landowner's grain growing right up to their doors. In six years, from 1964 to 1970, purchasing power went down to 75 percent of what it was for people who had next to nothing to start with. MacEoin concludes, "There seems to be no limit to what the poor can support. They simply develop a little less, physically and intellectually, die of hunger a little sooner." [5] Statistics, however, cannot capture the real feeling of desperation among the people as well as this poem from South America:

The Earth Is a Moon Satellite

Apollo 2 cost more than Apollo 1
Apollo 1 cost plenty.

Apollo 3 cost more than Apollo 2
Apollo 2 cost more than Apollo 1
Apollo 1 cost plenty.

Apollo 4 cost more than Apollo 3
Apollo 3 cost more than Apollo 2
Apollo 2 cost more than Apollo 1
Apollo 1 cost plenty.

Apollo 8 cost a fortune but nobody minded
because the astronauts were Protestants
and from the moon they read the Bible
to the delight and edification of Christians
and on their return Pope Paul gave them his blessing.

Apollo 9 cost more than all of them together
and that included Apollo 1 which cost plenty.

The great grandparents of the Acahualinca
people were less hungry than the grandparents.

The great grandparents died of hunger.

The grandparents of the Acahualinca people

were less hungry than the parents.

The grandparents died of hunger.

The parents of the Acahualinca people
were less hungry than the people are today.

The parents died of hunger.

The people who live today in Acahualinca
are less hungry than their children.

The children of the Acahualinca people
are not born because of hunger
and they hunger to be born
so they can die of hunger.

And that is what they do
they die of hunger.

Blessed are the poor
for they shall possess the moon.[6]

How can one appreciate the real violence of these conditions? Though not as stark in this country, the same dynamics of poverty exist. For most salaried people, prices rise faster than incomes, so they cut back in order to make ends meet. They buy cheaper cuts of meat, more chicken, or do without. What was once a daily item on the table becomes a luxury. For the Third World poor, bare survival is a difficult struggle.

The long-range consequences of hunger are alarming. Gary MacEoin suggests that hunger affects mental abilities, not only for a generation, but over several generations, and that the future projection is frightening:

> With a vast majority of the inhabitants of a region living generation after generation at a subhuman level, a deterioration in the quality of the stock is inevitable. In this perspective, the science fiction projection of a Chilean sociologist . . . acquires more plausibility. One cannot exclude the possibility that the world is heading for an evolutionary mutation, with some branches of the human race reaching upwards technologically and cyberneti-

cally to a new plateau, while others are destined to become "by the end of the century, the primitives of the civilized; and in the next century, the apes of a new humanity." [7]

This is too pessimistic a projection, because the human race, from what we know, has enormous staying power and adaptability. It is more likely that the wealthy countries will destroy one another first in the race to possess markets and resources.

The Violent Results of Wealth

One of the consequences of the inequality between rich and poor nations is the defensiveness and offensiveness of the wealthy nations. On the international level, the world spends $180 billion a year for arms.[8] It would be serious enough if the rich nations spent this money, but rulers in the poor nations also spend great amounts on arms. Weapons production and sales are good business. The demand is endless, because one can never have enough; one can arrange things so that "our side" must always have more, and thus keep the escalation going indefinitely.

In America alone, 41 cents out of every tax dollar goes directly to military programs, while another 18 cents goes toward payment on the national debt, created by war, as well as toward veterans' programs. In addition, for fiscal 1975, for the first time in our history, a peacetime military budget will rise and will be higher than our wartime military budget. Over the next two years, it is projected that we will spend $8 billion more than we do now.[9]

As a nation we are obsessed with security because inequality and maldistribution of wealth breed fear. The United States has far-flung military bases that ring the Soviet Union and China. Although the USSR has a larger army than the United States, with the exception of the ICBM's, its weaponry is defensive, whereas American weaponry is primarily offensive. *Our country leads the world in offensive power.*[10] A look at the amount we spend on war in the United States suggests how much we are committed to security. We spend far more of the federal budget on war-related items than on education, health, labor, and welfare programs. Sidney Lens, author of *The Military-Industrial Complex*, comments: "Convincing the American people that they ought to spend nine times as much on guns as on human welfare was an act of mesmerism by the military establishment without parallel." [11] Under Franklin Roosevelt, peacetime military budgets amounted to $600–$900 million yearly—and he was called a warmonger. Today's peacetime level is $90 billion, more than 100 times as much now as then.[12]

We are also preoccupied with our personal security, and for good reason. Daytime burglaries have risen 337 percent from 1960 to 1970. The Gallup Poll reports that one in six Americans in the suburbs or small towns does not feel safe at home. The suburbs are still considerably safer than the cities, but the suburbs are no longer safe havens of gracious living. Publicly people call for more "law and order" and privately they spend large amounts of money to protect their wealth. By 1980, it is estimated that the home protection industry alone may reach $400 million. "What this means is that within six years American homeowners who lose approximately $1600 million in property to thieves each year, may spend $1 on protection for each $4 of property stolen."[13] When wealth is unevenly distributed, the wealthy, like the foolish rich man in the parable (Luke 12:16–21), spend their riches not on the poor but on the police to protect their wealth.

Safety and health hazards on the job are a more serious form of hidden violence than street crime, though their perpetrators never are jailed. Ralph Nader claims:

> [These hazards] cause three times as many injuries as street crime: 15,000 sudden deaths last year, uncounted thousands of deaths resulting from occupational disease, 2.5 million disabling injuries, several million cases of less serious injuries and illness.[14]

When we think of violence, we usually mean open warfare or intentional, deliberate conflict. But structural or covert violence does considerably more harm to both poor and wealthy than war. Overcoming the wall of covert violence is the first step toward global shalom. The second step is preventing the poor from becoming dependent on our dangerous technology, which contains another form of hidden violence. Third World people should be able to control their own lives. Shalom is democratic decision-making.

THE VISION OF LIBERATION

The basic source of noncommunity in the contemporary world is not the division between East and West or between communist and capitalist nations. It is the division between colonizers and colonized. The new colonialism is one not of military empires in the old sense, but rather an economic colonialism. This new colonialism is the battleground of covert warfare, and conquest comes in a very different manner. John Foster Dulles is quoted as saying: "There are two ways of conquering a foreign nation. One is to gain control of its people by force of arms; the other is to gain control of its economy by financial means." [15]

The Development of Liberation Theology

In the 1960s, the watchword of the advanced industrial nations was "development" as this word applied to the poor nations of the world. The poor nations came to think of themselves as the Third World, belonging neither to the first world of Western Europe and North America nor to the second world of Russia and other communist nations. With the emergence of liberation movements in Africa, the failure of the Alliance for Progress in Latin America, and the long years of the Vietnam War, Third World countries have been engaged for many years in a struggle for their own liberation, rather than for development as defined by outsiders. For some countries, as in Africa in the 1950s and 1960s, liberation has meant independence from British, French, or Portuguese rule. In Southeast Asia, the struggle has been to throw off French rule, then U.S. domination.

Latin America won its political independence over a century ago. Now the need is to throw off the far more subtle domination of U.S. economic interests. It is a subtle kind of domination because economic conquest involves complex ties of dependence on the United States for parts for machinery, for bank loans, and for consumer goods resulting from new tastes developed by imported educational and mass media. A Latin American theologian points out that

> the poor countries are becoming ever more clearly aware that their underdevelopment is only the by-product of the development of other countries, because of the kind of relationship that exists between the rich and the poor countries. . . . Their own development will come about only with a struggle to break the domination of the rich countries.[16]

Yet this statement is also an oversimplification. Latin America's dependence on the United States is reciprocal. The ruling elites in Brazil, Argentina, and Colombia, to name but a few, themselves support this dependence of their countries on the United States. In turn, the United States maintains these groups in power, in the interests of political stability that protects U.S. business interests.[17] A government that would bring social justice in any Latin American country would need to redistribute the wealth of the feudal landowners and to appropriate the disproportionate share of wealth held by North American corporations as Chile under Allende did with the copper mines.

Theology of liberation expresses the same thrust for independence and self-determination that was expressed in the Old Testament by the story of liberation from Egypt in the book of Exodus, a basic model of liberation theology. But our own struggle for independence in the United States two hundred years ago is another model for the struggle of Latin American people.

What do Latin American theologians mean by liberation? First, they mean the power of people to create their own history, to have power over their own lives. In the Latin American context, this is likely to mean a socialist democracy, because Latin Americans have seen how capitalism in their country impoverishes the masses of people to benefit the few. Second, liberation means freedom for a full human development of the spirit. These theologians reject a consumption-oriented society like the United States as something obscene, because it

> produces and flaunts in an indecent way a suffocating abundance of material goods, while denying to its victims abroad, the basic needs of life; it is obscene when it gorges itself, when it accumulates heaps of garbage, while poisoning and burning the few edibles in the countries it wars on.[18]

These theologians envision in the liberation of the Third World the possibility of a new and humane social process, a world that will be seduced neither by the opulence of the first world nor by the rigidity of the second. They have seen the destructiveness of our aid, and many of them are simply saying, "Yanqui, go home." What these people—these Christians, Marxists, and humanists—insist on is space to create a new world, space free from North American aid or military intervention.

At the same time, we North Americans also have a vocation to help build a just and humane world. In North America, we too experience the need to be freed from the burdens of alienation from one another, from lack of power over our own lives. The Latin Americans remind us, however, that the process of liberation has certain priorities. Liberation involves both a cultural transformation in our own country as well as a social and political transformation. Emilio Castro, a Methodist bishop in Uruguay, describes the priorities thusly:

It is an evident fact that developed, or consumer, society tends to reify—to thing-ify—and massify man. And this challenges the Christian conscience to come up with imaginative ways to preclude such a mercantile utilization of man. But it is not true that this abuse is qualitatively or quantitatively comparable to the deprivation and marginalization, with their attendant hunger, ignorance and poverty, that are found in Latin America.[19]

Bishop Castro clearly puts the priority on eradicating hunger and poverty in Latin America, whereas North American liberation and cultural transformation clearly come second. The task is, however, two-pronged; both jobs have to be done simultaneously. Given the realities of American multinational corporations and their stranglehold over the Latin American continent, Latin Americans have no room for freedom until this hold is broken, a task for responsible North American Christians who hunger and thirst for justice at home. In turn, we cannot engage in this struggle without the help of our brothers and sisters south of the border.

The prospects for liberation at this moment of writing are bleak, especially since the fall of the Allende government in Chile. The magnitude of our job comes starkly into focus when we see an example of what we are up against in the downfall of Allende. Without overt intervention, forces in the United States were able to help bring Allende down by withholding loans and grants to the government but giving them instead to the military along with greatly increased military equipment. The ITT and the CIA have long acted behind the scenes.[20] Covert violence leads to overt violence.

Today, Latin America desperately needs liberation and social justice. Seventy percent of its 200 million people are subject to military rule.[21] Most of these military dictatorships are supported by economic aid, military training, and arms from the United States. The task before North Americans is to call off our big corporations and call off the government support of them as they work their will throughout the Third World with little or no regard for liberation of two-thirds of humanity.

ACTION FOR WORLD COMMUNITY

Where to Begin

The picture is depressing as long as we sit and pile up our statistics, but a defeatist attitude can be a self-fulfilling prophecy. If we begin where we are, begin to be concerned, begin to make our voices heard, we still have a chance to change the way things are.

At the highest level, governments can take action. Some countries, notably Canada and the Netherlands, have already pledged to contribute to international development 1 percent of their Gross National Product (GNP).[22] For the United States, 1 percent of our GNP would be about $10 billion, whereas we actually spend only half that amount in aid. Of this about two-fifths is direct military aid. Other aid is given in the form of loans.

One of the problems of direct government aid, however, is that very large sums of money may go into the wrong pockets. If the existing government is a military regime, concerned to imitate the wealthy countries, its development program will look good; but there will be little positive impact on the people. There are ways in which the U.S. government through the Agency for International Development (AID) does in fact fund many smaller projects at the grass roots level. Churches also do a good deal on the local level and could do more to help people set up their own farm cooperatives, food production units, and the like.

At the nongovernmental level of voluntary organizations, we can probably help the most. Unfortunately, such groups are decreasing in importance, while power gets concentrated in larger and larger units in federal and state government and in giant corporations. People's loyalties go more to the very large, the nation, and to the very small, the family. Churches seem to be one of the last forms of intermediate organization that might protest inhumanity and help people take power over their own concerns.

As noted earlier, in Brazil the military government has systematically attempted to destroy the voluntary organizations' independence and power by putting them under government control and by infiltrating them with secret agents. Trade unions, student organizations, peasant unions, professional organizations—none of these has any independent existence in Brazil. Today the church survives in Brazil only because it has been domesticated.

One of the most urgent areas of concern is an emergency program of food distribution, sustained over a long period. Churches, civic groups, and governments are usually generous in the face of the violence of earthquakes and floods; yet the covert violence of hunger is even more serious. Together with short-run distribution of food is the need for long-term food production, so that poor nations can begin to feed their own people. Instead of infusion of capital into enterprises like Exxon in Venezuela or Anaconda when it was in Chile, where the bulk of the profits goes back to the investors, a new kind of investment is needed—investment for social purposes, an investment in people. With the infusion of relatively small amounts of capital, people can meet their own needs for food, housing, sewage, and the like. As they develop this investment, they will in turn be able to produce more, to help other nations.

How will these countries become self-sufficient, self-governing, and fully liberated? The poor nations are in the process of undergoing their own industrial revolution, but they do not have the time for the kind of hit-and-miss pattern that Western Europe and the United States followed. Their revolution will need careful planning and the concerted effort of a whole people. The suffering that the Industrial Revolution caused in the West is easily forgotten because of its obvious rewards in the twentieth century. By contrast, the suffering endured in countries like Russia or China in the struggle to industrialize is better known. Yet Russia has performed a kind of economic miracle of industrialization within fifty-five years. Russia today boasts a per capita income of $1,000. China too is making great strides, though its per capita income is only $86. Yet China is doing an incredible job of supplying her people with food, housing, and education.

When we look at the covert violence of poverty, hunger, and powerlessness without assuming that our way is the only way to liberation, we can see why many Third World nations are choosing some form of socialism when they are allowed to elect their governments. It also helps us understand the desperation and the wisdom of theologians of liberation who see the shalom Jesus preached to be found not in the development but in the liberation of the oppressed (Luke 4:18).

Taking the First Steps

What does this analysis of international poverty have to do with individual Christians seeking a shalom community? After all, we are only individuals who have little enough power over our own lives. Even if we do have the global view and understand ourselves to be part of the body of Christ, linked to the world, we are still frustrated at how little we can do.

Christians consistently have had a strong sense of the need of people in other countries. In the past we have attempted to help by sending missionaries to carry the good news of the gospel. Recently, however, many people have become uncomfortable with the attempt to win converts in other lands. To impose the gospel in an uncritical way may be to destroy a whole culture. In the past, Christianity often has been imperialistic, because it lacked a basic respect for the people it came to serve and for the culture they had created. By now, however, many church people have gone to the opposite extreme by distrusting missions altogether.

A NEW UNDERSTANDING OF MISSION

The time is ripe to reexamine the missionary enterprise. We can say that it is no longer a question of *talking about Jesus* to the rest of the world, but rather a question of *being Jesus*—that is, doing what Jesus did according to the resources of knowledge and of wealth that we have today. Today's missionary faces a much more complex situation than his or her predecessor. The best missionaries have gone into other countries to participate in the life and work of the people, to be *with* them. Even when they have gone to a country on a short-term basis of intensive involvement, some have stayed to become citizens of their adopted country. They have attempted to understand its political, economic, and social structure as well as its language, religion, and communities. They see these things as a whole. Their concern is to help people see a new possibility of power to overcome the covert violence in their lives. Catholic missioners Father Tom Melville and Sister Peter (later Marjorie Melville), for example, worked with the peasants in Guatemala, assisted by a team of students. Gradually they became convinced that the people could make substantial gains only if they would become organized. As soon as the people organized, however, terrorists would shoot down the leaders one by one, while the ruling military dictatorship looked the other way. The Melvilles report that some 1400 peasant leaders were shot during the years they were there.[23] A Presbyterian missionary, Richard Shaull, came to a similar realization of the need for a new social process in Colombia and Brazil and, over the years in dialogue with Latin American churchmen themselves, developed a theology of social transformation. Like Paulo Freire, he became so well known and influential in Brazil that he was invited to leave by the military regime.

To do the work of Jesus is far more than preaching a word. It is acting out a message. "Word" means both change and action, and a minister of the gospel must know the whole complex reality of the culture to which he or she comes. This will require a study of anthropology, of culture, of language, but also of the economic and political situation of the country. The first years in the country may be simply a time of being there, of making contact, and of keeping in touch with people at home. The missionary is thus a person who lives in two worlds, but can also provide a place of contact where these worlds meet.

Two programs of mission already are serving these needs. One is the Frontier Intern program set up by the World Christian Student Federation. The aim initially was to send young people to a country in Africa, Asia, or Latin America. More recently, this group has come to believe that the United States, in the broad sense of mission outlined above, is itself a mission country. The United States itself can learn something of the human richness of other cultures by having Latin American or African or Asian Christians come to this country. The missionary movement today is dialogical.[24]

The other program involves a group of ecumenical lay Christians, Technoserve, founded in 1969 to assist people in less developed countries so that they can begin to create a new kind of action and productivity where they are. Recognizing that the initial problem is the infusion of sufficient capital to begin cooperative farming or a local factory, Technoserve provides the capital as a long-term loan at minimal interest rates, together with expertise. The purpose is to develop work cooperatives that use the resources most plentiful in the area, especially the resource of people. Unlike much of American investment that sets up business concerns along the American pattern, Technoserve attempts to fit a workable profit-making enterprise into the people's own value systems and way of life. Thus the people themselves become involved and are concerned to make the project work. The initial investment is returned to the nonprofit organization to be used for still other development projects. In this case, the well-known snowballing effect of profit is used directly for development.[25]

PARTICIPATION IN BUILDING GLOBAL SHALOM

Most of us, however, do not immediately have such options available. For each of us as Christians, a life-style of caring and sharing is not something that we can move toward very easily. We experience enormous pressures to earn more and spend more, even though we see the irrationality of such compulsive living. Yet we can begin on a personal level by "deconditioning" ourselves—that is, stopping ourselves from wanting all the luxuries we have been conditioned to want. Then we can work together with others to free ourselves from dependence on so much income and so many consumer goods. Instead of spending money on Christmas gifts and other excessive needs, we can begin to invest surplus money (money beyond our bare necessities) in Third World liberation. In creating a surplus, even out of our own necessities, we ourselves will have a new sense of power and worth, a sense of being linked to others who are making significant changes in their lives.

We have all been conditioned to think that everything must go up indefinitely—the standard of living, wages, enjoyment of goods. We know of people making $50,000 a year who still feel poor because this is not enough to meet their constantly escalating needs. The personal benefit of deconditioning at this level functions to create not only a surplus that can be used for others but a sense of freedom for oneself. The endless payments that come due every month—the mortgage on the house, the second car, payments on endless credit accounts and on other loans—all these can lock us into a life that has no room for neighbors, let alone the Third World. The average standard of living for the middle-class family particularly enslaves the father provider, as we have noted in Chapter 3.

We assume that the standard of living must go up, and that this upward direction is irreversible. This is not so! A depression can wipe out the gains of a whole generation. But it is also possible for a family or a community to deliberately de-escalate their standard of living, to de-consumerize their lives and thereby take the first steps of liberation from dependence.

It would be a mistake to expect the poor either in Latin America or in our own country to remain passive. They have experienced the covert violence of poverty, hunger, and unemployment; but they are a tough and resourceful people, too. Paulo Freire discovered the energy and creativity of the Brazilian peasants, but he was not alone. In the slums of São Paulo, a young woman, Carolina Maria de Jesus, was determined to become a writer in spite of incredible poverty and hardship. She learned to read and write, and a whole new world opened up to her. She was independent and tough, and refused both prostitution and marriage because they would make her dependent upon men, a dependence all the greater because of her own poverty. Without a job, like so many others in the slums of the large cities, she lived on what she could scavenge or beg for herself and her children. After a long day, often half sick, she wrote stories of the rich whose lives she imagined. In a journal she also wrote of her own life: what it meant to be poor and yet have dignity. One day a reporter discovered her and found out that she wanted to be a writer. Her stories did not impress him, but her journal rang true. He persuaded her to let him have it published. It has been a best-seller in Brazil, and it has sold in the United States in a paperback edition. Whether she is an exception or not—she herself felt that her neighbors lacked energy and ambition to get ahead—she provides some new hope, small as that hope must be, for most of the poor in Brazil.[26]

CONCLUSION

As a Christian I find myself torn between bitter realism and incurable optimism. I see in the vision of global shalom the tantalizing possibility of overcoming the walls of hostility. It is here where the traditional view of "feminine" values of empathy and concern for others will mesh with the "masculine" values of strength, persistence, and technological know-how in the service of a new world. As we break down the artificial walls between the male and female values, we will also be freed from the tribal notions of a limited peace, a peace narrowly confined to private loyalties of family and corporation, or even to the national loyalty to country, forgetting the people of the world.

Today the challenge is to realize that the body of Christ is the body of humanity, not only the small tribe of Christians in the world. Of necessity we have to invent or rediscover the Christian concept of solidarity where the individual is transformed into a public person, conscious of his or her bonds to the whole of humanity, conscious of living in a global village. Of all people, Christians can most truly be world citizens and lovers of the world. (See John 3:16.) Theirs is an effective love in action. With a bias toward the poor, it seeks abundant life for all people, liberation of the oppressed, a public peace, and free choice of people to rule their own lives. The method we suggest is naming the problems we have in common, analyzing and picturing them so we can understand them, dreaming, and envisioning an alternative future, working actively for that future, reflecting on our action, and following it up with more insightful and effective action. This is one way to bring down the walls of hostility on the way to the vision of shalom.

NOTES

Chapter 1

1. From the introduction to *Revolutionary Priest, The Complete Writings and Messages of Camilo Torres* (New York: Random House, 1971) by John Gerassi, p. 28.

2. Germán Guzman, *Camilo Torres*, translated by John D. Ring (New York: Sheed & Ward, 1969).

3. Lewis Mumford, *The Story of Utopias* (New York: Boni & Liveright, 1922), p. 11.

4. Camilo Torres, *Revolutionary Writings* (New York: Herder & Herder, 1969), p. 127.

5. For further information on the Congregation for Reconciliation, contact Rev. Richard Righter, 1512 Cory Dr., Dayton, Ohio 45406.

6. This version of the *Magnificat* reinterpreted by Sarah Bentley. Used by permission.

7. Elizabeth O'Connor, *Eighth Day of Creation, Gifts and Creativity* (Waco, Texas: Word Books, 1971), p. 52. This entire book, on the theology and practice of the gifts of the Spirit, is worth reading. It grew out of Ms. O'Connor's involvement with the Church of the Saviour in Washington, D.C. Many of her ideas apply to educational styles as well as to alternatives in worship and to work.

Chapter 2

1. *"Respondeo etsi mutabor"* is the original form as the theologian Eugen Rosenstock-Huessy gives it in *Out of Revolution* (New York: William Morrow, 1938), pp. 740–741. I owe this quotation and the following one to my friend and colleague, Bruce Boston, of the Philadelphia Theological Community. See Bruce O. Boston, *"I Respond Although I Will Be Changed": The Life and Historical Thought of Eugen Rosenstock-Huessy* (Ph.D. dissertation, Princeton Theological Seminary, 1963).

2. Eugen Rosenstock-Huessy, *The Christian Future; or, The Modern Mind Outrun* (New York: Harper & Row, 1966), p. 229. Used by permission.

3. For background on the Latin American situation, I recommend Gary MacEoin, *Revolution Next Door, Latin America in the 1970's* (New York: Holt, Rinehart & Winston, 1971).

For an overall view of Paulo Freire's work with the peasants in the Northeast, see Thomas G. Sanders' booklet, *The Paulo Freire Method* (American Universities Fieldstaff Reports, June 1968). Paulo Freire's own writings, which describe the philosophy behind the method, are *Pedagogy of the Oppressed*, translated by Myra Bergman Ramos (New York: Herder & Herder, 1970). *Cultural Action for Freedom* (Cambridge, Mass.: Harvard Educational Review, 1970, monograph). *Education for Critical Consciousness* (New York: Seabury Press, 1973).

4. Freire, *Cultural Action for Freedom*, monograph, p. 22.

5. *Ibid.*, p. 23.

6. From *Pedagogy of the Oppressed* by Paulo Freire, p. 57ff. © 1970 by Paulo Freire. Used by permission of the publisher, The Seabury Press, New York.

7. *Ibid.*, p. 36. © 1970 by Paulo Freire. Used by permission of the publisher, The Seabury Press, New York.

8. Thomas G. Sanders, *The Paulo Freire Method* (American Universities Fieldstaff, Inc., Fieldstaff Reports TGS 1–68; Box 150, Hanover, N.H. 03755), p. 11.

9. See Saul Alinsky, *Reveille for Radicals* (New York: Vintage Books, 1946), and Frederik Pohl, *Practical Politics 1972: How To Make Politics and Politicians Work for You* (New York: Ballantine Books, 1971).

10. See *Pedagogy of the Oppressed* by Paulo Freire, pp. 51 and 137.

11. *Ibid.*, pp. 119–120. © 1970 by Paulo Freire. Used by permission of the publisher, The Seabury Press, New York.

12. See Robert A. Gallagher, "Ministry of the Laity as Agents of Institutional Change," *National Association of Ecumenical Staff Journal*, April, 1972.

Chapter 3

1. Alexis de Tocqueville, *Democracy in America, Part the Second: The Social Influence of Democracy*, revised by Francis Bowen, further corrected and edited by Phillips Bradley (New York: Alfred A. Knopf, 1935), pp. 201, 211. Used by permission.

2. Abigail McCarthy, *Private Faces, Public Places* (New York: Doubleday, 1972), p. 259.

3. Karl Barth, *On Marriage* (Philadelphia: Fortress Press, 1968), p. 15.

4. Jessie Bernard, *The Future of Marriage* (New York: Bantam Books, 1973), pp. 42–44.

5. Ashley Montagu, *The Natural Superiority of Women* (New York: Macmillan, 1953), p. 21. Used by permission.

6. Hendrik M. Ruitenbeek, *The Male Myth* (New York: Dell Publishing Co., 1966), p. 27.

7. See Barth, *On Marriage.*

8. Simone de Beauvoir, in her brilliant study *The Second Sex*, translated and edited by H. M. Parshley (New York, Bantam Books, 1961), points out how women throughout their education and, in fact, throughout their lives are put down—are made into a second sex with second-class citizenship. Equally brilliantly, Elizabeth Gould Davis documents the history of the race and its mothers in *The First Sex* (Baltimore, Maryland: Penguin Books, 1972).

Archeologists are beginning to discover the richness of matriarchal civilizations, so that history itself provides alternatives to the present patriarchal structure of society. The matriarchal societies not only were not primitive, but they were more highly developed than many later societies. Yet they also were societies of domination in their own way.

9. See, for example, Oscar Lewis, *The Children of Sanchez: Autobiography of a Mexican Family* (New York: Random House, 1961).

10. *The Philadelphia Inquirer*, March, 1973.

11. Michele Murray, "The Louds of Santa Barbara," *Commonweal* 98 (March 23, 1973): 60.

12. *The Doctors* by Martin Gross (New York: Random House, 1966), pp. 343–366.

13. John H. Knowles, "Where Doctors Fail," *Saturday Review* 53 (August 22, 1970): 21. The entire issue is devoted to the subject of improving health care in the United States.

14. Noam Chomsky, *American Power and the New Mandarins* (New York: Pantheon Books, 1969).

15. Gloria Emerson, "Arms and the Woman," *Harpers* 246 (April, 1973): 34–45. Emphasis mine.

16. Clarence Darrow, the famous criminal lawyer, put it this way in 1935: "I don't care what the profession or calling or business, a few persons take all the rewards, and the rest become hired men and women." Today the only difference is that the hired men and women are paid a little more than before. Letter from Clarence Darrow, October 31, 1935, published in *Student Lawyer* (September, 1972), p. 32.

17. Herbert Richardson, *Nun, Witch and Playmate: The Americanization of Sex* (New York: Harper & Row, 1971). Used by permission.

18. *Philadelphia Inquirer* report, December 10, 1972. The story is brought up to date by: Mary Augusta Rodgers, "A POW's Return: Reunion Between Strangers?" *Woman's Day*, August, 1973, p. 76. The crowning touch to the paradox of the child-mother image is that the husband calls his wife "Mummy" even in their first tender moments of reunion.

19. Nena and George O'Neill, *Open Marriage: A New Lifestyle for Couples* (New York: Avon Books, 1972).

20. Abigail McCarthy, *Private Faces, Public Places*, p. 204.

21. *Ibid.*, p. 435.

22. For the new look for women, see "Big Is Beautiful: Make the Most of the Most," *Woman's Day*, August, 1973, pp. 88ff. Many of the women's magazines are including more and more of the motifs of women's liberation without specific references to the movement itself. To me this indicates the impact of the change. The "movement" belongs to ordinary women, to women wherever they are.

23. Susan Sontag, "The Double Standard of Aging" *Saturday Review* (September 23, 1972). See also Vivian Gornick, *Women in Sexist Society* (New York: Basic Books, Inc., 1971).

24. G. William Domhoff, "The Feminine Half of the Upper Class," in *The*

Higher Circles: The Governing Class in America (New York: Vintage Books, 1971).

25. Vivian Gornick, "Why Radcliffe Women Are Afraid of Success," *New York Sunday Times Magazine*, January 14, 1973, p. 11.

26. As noted above, men also are conditioned to a similar kind of dependence in the army. In civilian life, the master or "husband" to whom total loyalty is owed is the company or the employer. Ordinarily men's emotional life in this respect is simplified, in that the employee or company man is not expected to love the man he depends on and whom he serves. One can also find this kind of dependence in church organizations.

27. Gustavo Gutierrez, *A Theology of Liberation: History, Politics and Salvation*, translated by Sister Caridad Inda and John Eagleson (Maryknoll, N.Y.: Orbis Books, 1973).

28. Boston Women's Health Book Collective, *Our Bodies, Ourselves* (New York: Simon and Schuster, 1973).

29. *Time*, "Private-Practice Nurses," March 12, 1973, p. 70.

30. Nena and George O'Neill, *Open Marriage*.

Chapter 4

1. Harvey Cox, "The Nuclear Family: An Overloaded Fuse," *National Catholic Reporter*, April 20, 1973. Reprinted with permission of the author and of the National Catholic Reporter, Box 281, Kansas City, Mo. 64141. See also *The Family, Communes and Utopian Societies*, edited by Sallie Teselle (New York: Harper & Row, 1972).

2. Richard Sennett, *The Uses of Disorder: Personal Identity and City Life* (New York: Vintage/Knopf), p. 62. Copyright 1970. Used by permission of Alfred A. Knopf, Inc.

3. Daniel Berrigan, "The Church and the Peacemaking Role" (unpublished transcript of tape sent to the Deering Consultation on Peace Mobilization, sponsored by the United Church Board for Homeland Ministries), p. 3.

4. Lucy Powell, "Women Are Equals," in *Creative Congregations: Tested Strategies for Today's Churches*, edited by Edgar R. Trexler (Nashville: Abingdon Press, 1972), p. 36.

5. There are many general works on the family and its history. Two that may be helpful are: Gerald R. Leslie, *The Family in Social Context* (New York: Oxford University Press, 1967) and Ralph H. Turner, *Family Interaction* (New York: John Wiley & Sons, 1970).

6. Sennett, *op. cit.*, p. 52. Philippe Ariés makes the same point in *Centuries of Childhood*, translated by Robert Baldick (New York: Alfred A. Knopf, 1962): "The concept of the family, the concept of class, and perhaps elsewhere the concept of race, appear as manifestation of the same intolerance towards variety, the same insistence on uniformity" (p. 415). Used by permission.

7. "The American Family: Future Uncertain," *Time*, December 28, 1970, p. 35. Used by permission.

8. These comments apply primarily to middle-class families. Upper-class families have relegated their responsibilities for their children to servants and to boarding schools. Working-class people and poor people have not had the resources to devote themselves as thoroughly to the job of bringing up their children. See Philippe Ariés in *Centuries of Childhood.*

9. From *The Female Eunuch* by Germaine Greer, pp. 63–64. Copyright 1971 by McGraw-Hill. Used with permission of McGraw-Hill Book Company.

10. R. D. Laing, *Sanity, Madness and the Family: Families of Schizophrenics* (New York: Basic Books, 1971).

11. Kenneth Keniston, *Young Radicals: Notes on Committed Youth* (New York: Harcourt, Brace & World, 1968).

12. From *The Female Eunuch* by Germaine Greer, p. 246. Copyright 1971 by McGraw-Hill. Used with permission of McGraw-Hill Book Company.

13. The communal tradition in Christian history has generally been underplayed and would well repay intensive study. As a start, see Maren Lockwood Carden *Oneida: Utopian Community to Modern Corporation* (New York: Harper & Row, 1971) and Victor Peters, *All Things Common: The Hutterian Way of Life* (Minneapolis: University of Minnesota Press, 1966). For a description of a contemporary commune as part of church life, see Denham Grierson, *Young People in Communal Living* (Philadelphia: Westminster Press, 1971).

14. Charles Antoine, *Church and Power in Brazil* (Maryknoll, N.Y.: Orbis Books, 1973).

15. Clovis R. Shepherd, *Small Groups: Some Sociological Perspectives* (San Francisco: Chandler Pub. Co., 1964) states: "The average ratio for normal groups [i.e. groups that continue to function] is around two instrumental [i.e., work-oriented] acts to each social-emotional act. Where the ratio is higher than two to one, it may mean that the group members are highly task oriented, are confronted with a job to do, possess consensus with respect to their work, and feel a necessity to accomplish the job quickly and efficiently. . . . [this higher ratio] may also mean that the group's members are anxious about their relations to each other, are convinced that social-emotional acts are inappropriate in the situation, or are behaving in ways which inhibit the expression of social-emotional acts" (pp. 32–33).

16. Eda LeShan, parent-educator and producer of her own TV show, "How Do Your Children Grow?" describes the universal human need for warm physical contact. She comments out of a crisis experience of her own (a thought which has echoed some of my own thinking): "And it suddenly seemed inhuman to me that we expect our children to sleep alone, with no one to cuddle, until they grow up and marry!" in "Love Is a Cuddle . . . or a Cuddly Toy," *Woman's Day* (Aug., 1973), pp. 63, 152–154.

17. Ministry in its present structures in Protestantism usually requires that the (male) minister be married. If the minister is female, she need not be married. It would be interesting to know what the assumptions are behind this difference in expectations. The Catholic priest's situation is the reverse of the Protestant minister's; he is required to be unmarried.

18. See Daniel Berrigan, "The Church and the Peacemaking Role," p. 67.

19. See also Thomas Gordon, *Parent Effectiveness Training: The No-Lose Program for Training Responsible Children* (New York: Peter H. Wyden, 1970).

20. Patricia Curtis, "We Live in a Commune," *Family Circle*, February, 1973, p. 50.

21. Reported by Mike Wallace on CBS's *Sixty Minutes*, 1972.

22. A. S. Neill, *Summerhill: A Radical Approach to Child Rearing* (New York: Hart Pub. Co., 1960).

23. *Plato's Republic*, translated by Benjamin Jowett (New York: Airmont Pub. Co., 1968).

Chapter 5

1. John Kenneth Galbraith, *The Affluent Society* (Boston: Houghton Mifflin Co., 1963), p. 133.

2. *Ibid.*, p. 134.

3. Joseph Heller's novel, *Catch-22* (New York: Simon and Schuster, 1961), depicted army life as a trap from which one could never escape. After one had fulfilled all the requirements of combat duty and time, there was still always "Catch-22" in the regulations, one more reason why one could not leave.

4. For example, the Teamsters have acted against Cesar Chavez and the United Farmworkers. The Teamsters' interests at this point are closer to the interests of the growers than of the Chicano workers.

5. Niall Brennan, *The Making of a Moron* (New York: Sheed & Ward, 1953).

6. In a recent issue of the *Bulletin of the Council for the Study of Religion*, two women theologians call attention to this style. It would seem that women, not having wives, can never compete with professional men(!). See Carol Christ and Judith Plaskow Goldenberg, "For the Advancement of My Career: A Form Critical Study in the Art of Acknowledgement," *BCSR 3* (1972): 10–14.

7. I use male language at this point by design, because I am describing what exists at the present time.

8. Betty Friedan, *The Feminine Mystique* (New York: W. W. Norton & Co., 1963).

9. John Kenneth Galbraith, *Economics and the Public Purpose* (Boston: Houghton Mifflin Co., 1973).

10. This idea of including young people in the ongoing life of society has been suggested by Ivan Illich for underdeveloped countries, but it would also work in the United States. See Ivan D. Illich, *Deschooling Society* (New York: Harper & Row, 1971).

11. See Everett Reimer, *School Is Dead: Alternatives in Education* (New York: Doubleday, 1971) and Herbert R. Zohl, *The Open Classroom: A Practical Guide to a New Way of Teaching* (New York: Random House, 1972).

12. For a description of the process of democratizing factory work, see Fred H. Blum, *Toward a Democratic Work Process: The Hormel-Packinghouse Workers' Experiment* (New York: Harper & Brothers, 1953). For a more recent book, see Charles Hampden-Turner, *Radical Man: The Process of Psycho-Social Development* (New York: Doubleday Anchor Books, 1971).

13. David Jenkins, "Industrial Democracy in Sweden," *The New York Times*, October 14, 1973.

14. Claudia Levy, "Everyone Gets a Share," *The Philadelphia Inquirer*, November 12, 1973.

Chapter 6

1. W. Warren Wagar, *Building the City of Man: Outlines of a World Civilization* (New York: Grossman Pub., 1971), p. 73.

2. The Brazilian theologian Rubem Alves also sees the work of negation to be essential to freedom. See *A Theology of Human Hope* (Washington, D.C.: Corpus, 1971).

3. Gustavo Gutierrez, *A Theology of Liberation: History, Politics and Salvation*, translated by Sister Caridad Inda and John Eagleson (Maryknoll, N.Y.: Orbis Books, 1973), p. 35.

4. See Ferdinand Lundberg, *The Rich and the Super Rich* (New York: Bantam Books, 1969).

5. G. William Domhoff, *The Higher Circles: The Governing Class in America* (New York: Vintage Books, 1971).

6. *Ibid.*, p. 106.

7. *Ibid.*, p. 107.

8. The National Welfare Rights Organization in cooperation with the United Church Board for Homeland Ministries. *Six Myths About Welfare*, 1971, p. 12. Statistics taken from the President's Commission on Income Maintenance Programs, *Poverty Amid Plenty: The American Paradox*, November, 1969.

9. *Ibid.*, p. 12.

10. Information taken from the pamphlet, *Take the Rich Off Welfare*, published by the Tax Action Campaign.

11. *Ibid.*

12. Citizens' Board of Inquiry into Hunger and Malnutrition in the United States, *Hunger U.S.A.* (Boston: Beacon Press, 1968). See also Michael Harrington, *The Other America: Poverty in the United States* (New York: Macmillan, 1970).

13. Timothy J. Sampson, *Welfare: A Handbook for Friend and Foe* (Philadelphia: Pilgrim Press, 1972).

14. *Six Myths About Welfare*, p. 12.

15. Report of a study for Office of Economic Opportunity by David Elesh and others from the University of Wisconsin, *Philadelphia Inquirer*, August 26, 1973.

16. Philip Slater, *The Pursuit of Loneliness: American Culture at the*

Breaking Point (Boston: Beacon Press, 1970), p. 15. Slater calls this disregard of people a "toilet assumption" whereby we flush out of society the unpleasant rejects.

17. "A Gauge for Well-Being," *Time*, April 9, 1973, p. 98.

18. Gustavo Gutierrez, *A Theology of Liberation*, pp. 294–295.

19. For further suggestions, see Edgar R. Trexler, editor, *Creative Congregations: Tested Strategies for Today's Churches* (Nashville: Abingdon Press, 1972). See also W. Ron Jones, *Finding Community: A Guide to Community Research and Action* (Palo Alto: James E. Freel and Associates, 577 College Avenue, Palo Alto, California, 1971).

20. Quoted in Sampson, *Welfare*, pp. 100–109. From "Weak on Welfare," *Barnard Alumnae*, Winter 1970. Used by permission.

21. See Denis Grierson, *Young People in Communal Living* (Philadelphia: Westminster Press, 1971).

22. Wolf Von Eckadt, "A Fresh Scene in the Clean Dream," *Saturday Review of the Society*, May 15, 1971, p. 21ff.

Chapter 7

1. Robert Theobald, *The Rich and the Poor: A Study of the Economics of Rising Expectations* (New York: Mentor Books, 1960), p. 18. Although the book is somewhat out of date, especially in its hopes for the Alliance for Progress in Latin America, it is well worth reading.

2. Reprinted from *The Lopsided World* by Barbara Ward, p. 12. By permission of W. W. Norton & Company, Inc. Copyright © 1968 by W. W. Norton & Company, Inc.

3. *Ibid.*, pp. 105–110.

4. Gary MacEoin, *Revolution Next Door: Latin America in the 1970's* (New York: Holt, Rinehart & Winston, 1971), p. 88.

5. *Ibid.*, p. 211.

6. Gary MacEoin, "Latin America: Who is to Blame?" *Commonweal* 94, No. 14 (June 25, 1971): 331. The poem is written by a Nicaraguan, Leonel Rugama, and was originally published in a student magazine in Montevideo, Uruguay.

7. MacEoin, *Revolution Next Door*, p. 212. No source is given for the brief quotation at the end.

8. Stockholm International Peace Research Institute, *SIPRI Yearbook of World Armaments and Disarmaments 1968/69* (New York: Humanities Press, 1970), p. 27.

9. In real dollars, the amount will be somewhat less at present rates of inflation.

10. See Sidney Lens, *The Military-Industrial Complex* (Philadelphia: Pilgrim Press, 1970), p. 11. *Information Please Almanac* figures suggest the same thing.

11. *Ibid.*, p. 1. See also the CBS Documentary, *The Selling of the Pentagon* (52 minutes, rental fee $17.50 from Office for Audio-Visuals, UCC

(rentals), 600 Grand Avenue, Ridgefield, N.J. 07657; or 512 Burlington Avenue, LaGrange, Ill. 60525.

12. *Ibid.*, p. 11.

13. Charles N. Barnard, "The Fortification of Suburbia Against the Burglar in the Bushes," *Saturday Review of the Society*, May, 1973, p. 38.

14. Ralph Nader, *Unsafe at Any Speed: The Designed-In Dangers of the American Automobile* (New York: Bantam Books, 1972).

15. Quoted in *The Enemy* by Felix Green (New York: Vintage Books, 1971), p. 153.

16. Gustavo Gutierrez, *A Theology of Liberation: History, Politics and Salvation*, translated by Sister Caridad Inda and John Eagleson (Maryknoll, N.Y.: Orbis Books, 1973), p. 26.

17. See Helen Jaworski, "The Integrated Structures of Dependence and Domination in the Americas," *Freedom and Unfreedom in the Americas: Towards a Theology of Liberation*, edited by Thomas E. Quigley (New York: IDOC Books, 1971), p. 21.

18. Alex Morelli, "Man Liberated from Sin and Oppression: A Theology of Liberation," in *Freedom and Unfreedom in the Americas*, p. 82.

19. Emilio Castro, "A Call to Action," *Freedom and Unfreedom in the Americas*, pp. 44–45.

20. See "After the Fall," *Time*, September 24, 1973, pp. 35–46, and "Mrs. Allende Confirms Husband Killed Himself," *New York Times*, Sunday, September 16, 1973.

21. "The Bloody End of a Marxist Dream," *Time*, September 24, 1973, p. 46.

22. Ward, *The Lopsided World*, p. 13.

23. The so-called terrorists operated with tacit approval of the Guatemalan government. See Tom and Marjorie Melville, *Whose Heaven, Whose Earth?* (New York: Knopf, 1971).

24. For further information, contact Margaret Flory, Frontier Intern Program, World Christian Student Federation, 475 Riverside Drive, New York, N.Y. 10027.

25. It is worth noting also that this form of nonprofit organization also functions as a work alternative to the dominant business world. It provides people with a way of using business skills to do work that is in itself socially productive.

At one point, the members of the organization became aware that it had become bureaucratic in spite of its small size and its ideology. To show that these processes are not irreversible, the group set out to "debureaucratize" its procedures. Written reports in triplicate are down to a minimum, while personal contact between members and group decision-making provide both personal accountability and flexibility.

26. Carolina Maria de Jesus, *Child of the Dark: The Diary of Carolina Maria de Jesus*, translated by David St. Clair (New York: Signet Books, 1962).

ADDITIONAL READINGS

Most of the following books are available from your denominational or local bookstore. Check your local library for magazines and for out of print books.

Chapter 1

David E. Babin, *The Celebration of Life,* Our Changing Liturgy (New York: Morehouse-Barlow, 1969).

Myron B. Bloy, Jr., *Multi-Media Worship*: A Model and Nine Viewpoints (New York: Seabury Press, 1969).

Mordecai L. Brill, Marlene Halpin, William H. Genné, *Write Your Own Wedding*: A Personal Guide for Couples of All Faiths (New York: Association Press, 1973).

John Pairman Brown and Richard L. York, *The Covenant of Peace*: A Liberation Prayer Book, by the Free Church of Berkeley (New York: Morehouse-Barlow, 1971).

Harvey Cox, *The Feast of Fools*, A Theological Essay on Festivity and Fantasy (Cambridge: Harvard University Press, 1969).

Gabriel Fackre, *Humiliation and Celebration*: Post-Radical Themes in Doctrine, Morals, and Mission (New York: Sheed and Ward, 1969).

Clifford Frazier and Anthony Meyer, *Discovery in Drama* (Paramus, N.J.: Paulist Press, 1969).

Robert J. Heyer and Richard J. Payne, *Discovery in Prayer* (Paramus, N.J.: Paulist Press, 1969).

Robert F. Hoey, ed., *The Experimental Liturgy Book* (New York: Herder and Herder, 1969).

Sam Keen, *To a Dancing God* (New York: Harper and Row, 1970).

Elizabeth O'Connor, *Eighth Day of Creation*: Gifts and Creativity (Waco, Texas: Word Books, Publisher, 1971).

Clarence J. Rivers, *Celebration* (New York: Herder and Herder, 1969).

Jay C. Rochelle, *The Revolutionary Year:* Recapturing the Meaning of the Christian Year (Philadelphia: Fortress Press, 1973).

Jerry Silverman, *The Liberated Woman's Songbook* (New York: Collier Books, 1971).

Ross Snyder, *Contemporary Celebration* (Nashville: Abingdon Press, 1971).

Chapter 2

Clovis R. Shepherd, *Small Groups* (Scranton, Pennsylvania: Chandler Publishing Company, Inc., 1964).

Sidney B. Simon *et al.*, *Values Clarification*: A Handbook of Practical Strategies for Teachers and Students (New York: Hart Publishing Company, Inc., 1972).

Herbert A. Thelen, *Dynamics of Groups at Work* (Chicago and London: University of Chicago Press, 1954, 1970).

Edgar R. Trexler, ed., *Creative Congregations*: Tested Strategies for Today's Churches (Nashville: Abingdon Press, 1972).

Elizabeth Flynn and John F. La Faso, *Group Discussion as Learning Process*: A Sourcebook (Paramus, N.J.: Paulist Press, 1972).

Chapter 3

Pamela Allen, *Free Space* (Washington, N.J.: Times Change, 1971).

Jessie Bernard, *The Future of Marriage* (New York: Bantam Books, 1973).

Simone de Beauvoir, *The Second Sex* (Translated and edited by H. M. Parshley; New York: Bantam Books, 1961).

Elizabeth Gould Davis, *The First Sex* (Baltimore, Maryland: Penguin Books, Inc., 1972).

Doely, Sarah Bentley, *Women's Liberation and the Church* (New York: Association Press, 1970).

G. William Domhoff, "The Feminine Half of the Upper Class" in *The Higher Circles*: The Governing Class in America (New York: Vintage Books, 1971).

Eve 'N Us, Filmstrip on Images and Roles of Women in the Church. Order from The Service Center, 7820 Reading Road, Cincinnati, Ohio 45237.

Vivian Gornick, "Why Radcliffe Women Are Afraid of Success," *New York Sunday Times Magazine*, January 14, 1973.

Vivian Gornick and Barbara K. Moran, *Woman in Sexist Society*, Studies in Power and Powerlessness (New York: New American Library, 1972).

Chapter 4

Rubem Alves, *Tomorrow's Child:* Imagination, Creativity and the Rebirth of Culture (New York: Harper and Row, 1972).

Daniel Berrigan, *The Geography of Faith*: Conversations Between Daniel Berrigan When Underground and Robert Coles (Boston: Beacon Press, 1971).

Richard Fairfield, *Communes, U.S.A.*: A Personal Tour (Baltimore, Maryland: Penguin Books, 1972).

Ludwig Feuer, *The Conflict of Generations*: The Character and Significance of Student Movements (New York: Basic Books, 1969).

David Finkelhor, "Boston Area Communes," IDOC (International Documentation North American Edition), October 30, 1971, pp. 3–27.

Edward T. Hall, *The Hidden Dimension* (New York: Anchor Books, 1969).

IDOC, "New Forms of Community," March 25, 1972. There are several articles on communities of Christians in different parts of the world in this issue. (Subscription address: IDOC, c/o Service Center, 7820 Reading Road, Cincinnati, Ohio 45237.)

R. D. Laing, *The Politics of the Family and Other Essays* (London: Tavistock Publications, 1971).

Raymond L. Muncy, *Sex and Marriage in Utopian Communities,* 19th Century America (Bloomington: Indiana University Press, 1973).

Ron E. Roberts, *The New Communes*: Coming Together in America (Englewood Cliffs, N.J.: Prentice-Hall, Inc., 1971).

Chapter 5

Rubem Alves, *A Theology of Human Hope* (St. Meinrad, Ind.: Abbey Press, 1972).

Fred H. Blum, *Toward a Democratic Work Process*, The Hormel-Packinghouse Workers' Experiment (New York: Harper and Brothers, 1953).

Kenneth Lasson, *The Workers:* Portraits of Nine American Job Holders, with an Afterword by Ralph Nader (New York: Bantam Books, 1972).

C. Wright Mills, *White Collar*: The American Middle Classes (New York: Oxford University Press, 1956).

John Oliver Nelson, ed., *Work and Vocation*: A Christian Discussion (New York: Harper and Brothers, 1954).

Philip E. Slater, *The Pursuit of Loneliness*: American Culture at the Breaking Point (Boston: Beacon Press, 1970).

Erwin O. Smigel, *Work and Leisure*: A Contemporary Social Problem (New Haven, Conn.: College and University Press, 1963).

Robert Theobald, *Free Men and Free Markets* (Garden City, N.Y.: Doubleday Anchor Books, 1965).

William H. Whyte, Jr., *The Organization Man* (Garden City, N.Y.: Doubleday Anchor Books, 1957).

Ferdynand Zweig, *The Worker in an Affluent Society*: Family Life and Industry (New York: The Free Press of Glencoe, Inc., 1961).

Chapter 6

Benjamin Chinitz, ed., *City and Suburb*: The Economics of Metropolitan Growth (Englewood Cliffs, N.J.: Prentice-Hall, Inc., 1964).

Harvey Cox, *The Secular City* (New York: The Macmillan Company, 1965).

N. J. Demerath, III, *Social Class in American Protestantism* (Chicago: Rand McNally and Company, 1965).

Ford Foundation Policy Paper, *Community Development Corporations*: A Strategy for Depressed Urban and Rural Areas, 1973).

John Kenneth Galbraith, *The Affluent Society* (Boston: Houghton Mifflin Company, 1963).

Lawrence Haworth, *The Good City* (Bloomington, Ind.: Indiana University Press, 1966).

Morris Janowitz, *The Community Press in an Urban Setting*: The Social Elements of Urbanism (Chicago: University of Chicago Press, 1967).
Ralph Nader, *et al.*, *Whistle Blowing*: Report of the Conference on Professional Responsibility (New York: Bantam Books, 1972).
Walter Rauschenbusch, *A Theology for the Social Gospel* (Nashville: Abingdon Press, 1917).
Theodore Roszak, *Where the Wasteland Ends*: Politics and Transcendence in Postindustrial Society (Garden City, N.Y.: Doubleday Anchor Books, 1973).
Jean-Jacques Servan-Schreiber, *The Radical Alternative* (New York: Dell Publishing Company, 1971).
Alvin Toffler, *The Culture Consumers*: Art and Affluence in America (Baltimore, Md.: Penguin Books, 1965).
Arnold Toynbee, *Surviving the Future* (New York: Oxford University Press, 1971).
Sam Bass Warner, Jr., ed., *Planning for a Nation of Cities* (Cambridge: M.I.T. Press, 1966).
Gibson Winter, *The New Creation as Metropolis* (New York: The Macmillan Company, 1963).

Chapter 7

Rubem Alves, *A Theology of Human Hope* (St. Meinrad, Ind.: Abbey Press, 1972).
———, *Tomorrow's Child*: Imagination, Creativity and the Rebirth of Culture (New York: Harper and Row, 1972).
Richard J. Barnet, *The Economy of Death* (New York: Atheneum, 1969).
Franz Bockle, ed., *The Social Message of the Gospels*, Concilium Volume 35 (Paramus, N.J.: Paulist Press, 1968).
Louis Colonnese, ed., *Conscientization for Liberation* (Washington, D.C.: Division for Latin America, U.S. Catholic Conference, 1971). This book is a collection of papers given at the Catholic Interamerican Cooperation Program (CICOP) conference of 1970.
James H. Cone, *Black Theology and Black Power* (New York: Seabury Press, 1969).
Council on Economic Priorities, *Efficiency in Death*: The Manufacturers of Anti-Personnel Weapons (New York: Harper and Row, 1970).
Frantz Fanon, *Black Skin, White Masks*: The Experiences of a Black Man in a White World, trans. by Charles Lam Markmann (New York: Grove Press, Inc., 1967).
———, *The Wretched of the Earth*, trans. by Constance Farrington (New York: Grove Press, Inc., 1968).
Paulo Freire, *Education for a Critical Consciousness* (New York: Seabury Press, 1973).
———, *Pedagogy of the Oppressed*, trans. by Myra Bergman Ramos (New York: Herder and Herder, 1970).
Gustavo Gutierrez, *A Theology of Liberation*: History, Politics and Salvation,

trans. Sister Caridad Inda and John Eagleson (Maryknoll, New York: Orbis Books, 1973).

Albert T. Hirschman, "How to Divest in Latin America and Why," *Cross Currents* 21 (1971), pp. 320–333.

François Houtart and André Rousseau, *The Church and Revolution*, trans. Violet Nevile (Maryknoll, N.Y.: Orbis Books, 1971).

IDOC (International Documentation Service), *When All Else Fails*: Christian Arguments on Violent Revolution (Philadelphia: United Church Press, 1970).

Peter Kapenga, "Changes Essential to Close the Gap Between Rich, Poor Nations," FCNL Washington Newsletter (July, 1972), No. 339.

Ernest Käsemann, *Jesus Means Freedom*, trans. Frank Clarke (Philadelphia: Fortress Press, 1968).

Gary MacEoin, ed., *Latin America in Search of Liberation*, Special Issue of *Cross Currents* 21 (Summer 1971).

Donella H. Meadows *et al.*, *The Limits to Growth*: A Report for the Club of Rome's Project on the Predicament of Mankind (New York: Universe Books, 1972).

Albert Memmi, *Dominated Man*: Notes Toward a Portrait (New York: Orion Press, 1968). There is also a chapter on "The Woman."

James Petras and Maurice Zeitlin, eds., *Latin America*: Reform or Revolution? A Reader (New York: Fawcett World, 1973).

Camilo Torres, *Revolutionary Priest*, The Complete Writings and Messages of Camilo Torres, ed. John Gerassi (New York: Random House, 1971).

United Nations, *Economic Bulletin for Latin America*, No. 13 (November, 1968).

UNITED CHURCH PRESS
PHILADELPHIA

ISBN 0-8298-02